*sixth edition*

# Method of Organ Playing

**HAROLD GLEASON**

PRENTICE-HALL, INC., Englewood Cliffs, New Jersey 07632

*Library of Congress Cataloging in Publication Data*

GLEASON, HAROLD (date)
  Method of organ playing.

  Principally exercises.
  Bibliography: p.
  1. Organ—Methods.  I. Title.
MT182.G55     786.7     78-17101
ISBN  0-13-579466-8

Printed in the United States of America

10  9  8  7  6  5  4  3  2  1

Editorial/production supervision by Fred Bernardi
Page layout by Gail Collis
Manufacturing buyer: Ed Leone

PRENTICE-HALL INTERNATIONAL, INC., *London*
PRENTICE-HALL OF AUSTRALIA PTY. LIMITED, *Sydney*
PRENTICE-HALL OF CANADA, LTD., *Toronto*
PRENTICE-HALL OF INDIA PRIVATE LIMITED, *New Delhi*
PRENTICE-HALL OF JAPAN, INC., *Tokyo*
PRENTICE-HALL OF SOUTHEAST ASIA PTE. LTD., *Singapore*
WHITEHALL BOOKS LIMITED, *Wellington, New Zealand*

To My Wife

# Contents

**Part Five**

**PEDAL TECHNIQUE AND PEDAL EXERCISES**

**Part Six**

**STUDIES AND COMPOSITIONS FOR MANUALS AND PEDAL**

**Part Seven**

**SERVICE PLAYING**

**Part Eight**

**SCALES FOR MANUALS AND PEDALS**

## APPENDICES

## COMPOSITIONS FOR MANUALS IN PART FOUR

## COMPOSITIONS FOR MANUALS AND PEDALS IN PART SIX

# Preface

The sixth edition of *Method of Organ Playing* includes extensive new material and revisions of the text and music. The "Bibliographies" have been brought up to date, the "Organ Specifications" have been revised and new ones added. The "Graded Course in Organ Playing" has been revised and more contemporary compositions are included.

New sections include "Performance Practice" from the sixteenth century through the Baroque, "Service Playing," and "Learning Techniques."

The section on "Registration" has been completely revised and enlarged.

A few new compositions have been included, and some have been re-edited to give indications for performance with *notes inégales,* early fingerings, articulations, and embellishments.

The principles of technique and interpretation presented in this edition and earlier editions are based on thirty-five years of experience as a teacher of organ playing at the Eastman School of Music of the University of Rochester, years of research, and training with teachers representing various schools of organ playing. These teachers include Ernest Douglas (German), Edwin Lemare (English), Lynnwood Farnam (Canadian-American), and Joseph Bonnet (French).

## ACKNOWLEDGMENTS

I am greatly indebted to my wife, Catharine Crozier Gleason, for her contribution of articles on *"Notes Inégales,"* "Embellishment of Sixteenth-Century Music," as well as revisions in fingering and articulation in various compositions; for revising the "Graded Course in Organ Playing," "Organ Specifications," and "Bibliographies;" and for help in preparing this new edition for publication.

My sincere thanks to my colleagues, organists and teachers, who have made helpful suggestions, and especially to Orpha Ochse and Warren Becker for their help in proofreading and preparing the manuscript, and to Frederick Swann for suggestions in regard to the section on *"Service Playing."* Also to the American composers, Wayne Barlow, Thomas Canning, Herbert Elwell, Herbert Inch, Allen I. McHose and Leo Sowerby for original studies and compositions from the fifth edition of *Method of Organ Playing.*

My thanks and appreciation to the editors at Prentice-Hall for their care and patience in preparing and bringing this book into print.

Acknowledgment is made to the Library of the School of Music of Yale University for permission to reproduce the *Table of Ornaments, Applicatio* and *Praeludium* from W. F. Bach's *Clavier-Büchlein.*

The following have given permission to use music, excerpts of music, quotations, or organ specifications. These have also been acknowledged in footnotes.

Alfred Publishing Company
Belwin-Mills Publishing Corporation
Concordia Publishing House
Dover Publications
European American Music Distributors Corporation

Indiana University Press
W. W. Norton & Company
C. F. Peters Corporation
Lawrence Phelps and Associates
Theodore Presser Company
*Vereniging Voor Nederlandse Musiekgeschiedenis*

*San Diego, California*                                    HAROLD GLEASON

# *Introduction– The Organ– Registration*

# Introduction

The purpose of *Method of Organ Playing* is to provide the musical and technical foundation necessary for the mastery of the art of organ playing.

A "method" is an orderly process toward that goal and a way of achieving that goal in the most thorough and efficient manner. The basic principles of organ playing are fundamental, but the method of presenting these principles will vary with each student.

A well-grounded piano technique is essential for the beginning organ student, and it is impossible to achieve real proficiency without it. The study of organ playing should not begin until the student has mastered a repertoire which includes Bach's Two- and Three-part Inventions, some of *The Well-Tempered Clavier* and easier sonatas by Haydn, Mozart, and Beethoven.

*Method of Organ Playing* is not organized in a series of lessons, but is divided into two large sections with four parts in each section.

### Section I

Part I:   Introduction—The Organ— Registration

Part II:   Performance Practice: Ornamentation —Embellishment of Sixteenth-Century Music—*Notes Inégales*—Fingering— Touch—Phrasing—Articulation— *Affektenlehre*—Tempo Rubato—Style and Interpretation

Part III:   Manual Technique and Manual Exercises—Part Playing

Part IV:   Learning Techniques: Practicing— Fingering—Touch—Accents— Memorizing
Compositions for Manuals

### Section II

Part V:   Pedal Technique

Part VI:   Compositions for Manuals and Pedal

Part VII:   Service Playing

Part VIII:   Scales for Manuals and Pedal

Appendices:   Graded Course in Organ Playing— Organ Specifications—Organ Music of the Renaissance and Baroque— Bibliography (Books-Articles) — Illustrations.

The variety and extent of the technical exercises and compositions will enable the teacher to select those best suited to the needs of each student. The student should complete a substantial number of the compositions in *Method of Organ Playing* before beginning the study of music in the "Graded Course in Organ Playing" (Appendix A).

The student's first lessons may well begin with "Manual Technique and Manual Exercises," page 61. The study of The Organ, Registration, Performance Practice, and also harmony, counterpoint, the history of organ literature, and Service Playing should be gradually integrated into the student's training.

All the music in *Method of Organ Playing* is of high quality and will form the foundation for continued study, not only of great organ music, but of outstanding works in the fields of piano, chamber, orchestral, and choral music.

All art requires a lifetime of study, and no concept of a work of art is final.

# The Organ

## GENERAL DESCRIPTION

The study of the history and construction of the organ may well begin with the first lessons. There are many books dealing in detail with this subject, and the student should consult the bibliography in Appendix D. The following brief description of the contemporary organ will serve as an introduction to further study.

The organ is a wind instrument played from a keyboard. It consists of a series of pipes placed on a wind chest supplied with valves under the pipes. These valves are operated by the keys through electro-pneumatic action, through mechanical means (trackers), or through direct electric action.

A constant supply of air at steady pressure must be delivered to the wind chest. This is usually accomplished today by means of an electric blower and a reservoir (formerly a bellows). The air is blown into the reservoir, the top of which is weighted or sprung in order to keep the wind at a steady pressure. It is then delivered from the reservoir to the wind chests through a wind pipe.

Each division of the organ contains a number of sets or ranks of pipes of varying qualities and pitches. There is one pipe (except in mixtures) for each of the sixty-one notes of the standard keyboard. These ranks are controlled by knobs or tablets called "stops" because originally the knobs were used to "stop" the rank of pipes from sounding (speaking). The terms "stop" and "register" are also used for a complete rank of pipes. The sounding of a pipe requires two basic operations:

1.  The desired stop-knob is drawn, admitting the wind under that rank of pipes.
2.  The key is depressed, causing the pallet (valve) to open and admit the wind to the pipe.

The organ may consist of one keyboard or as many as five keyboards. Normally, an organ will have from two to four manual keyboards and a pedal keyboard.

Each manual keyboard has a compass of 61 notes, extending from C to c⁴. The pedal board has 32 notes extending from C to g¹. A mechanical-action organ may have a smaller compass for the manuals and pedal.

The compass of the organ, however, is much greater than that of its keyboards. Stops sounding as much as two octaves below and three octaves above the normal or piano pitch are found on larger organs, giving the instrument a full compass of over nine octaves.

The different octaves will always be indicated as follows:

A stop of normal (unison) pitch is indicated by the symbol 8' (eight-foot). This term was derived from the fact that the low C of an open pipe is approximately eight feet long. If the low C pipe is 16' long, the entire stop will sound one octave lower than the 8' pitch. Similarly, stops indicated by the symbols 4', 2', 1' will sound one octave, two octaves, three octaves, respectively, above the unison pitch of the note played.

In addition to the various unison and octave pitches, there are stops known as mutations with pitches which correspond to the off-unison partials (2⅔', 1⅗', 1⅓', and rarely, 1⅐'). These sound respectively 12, 17, 19, and 21 scale notes above the unison pitch of the note played. There are also stops known as mixtures which comprise both unison and off-unison partials. Mutations, mixtures, and partials will be explained in more detail below.

Each keyboard (manual) represents a separate division or organ which is more or less complete in itself. The order and the names of the keyboards vary in different countries, and the compass of the manuals and pedal may be shorter than in the United States.

Specifications of organs from the sixteenth century to the twentieth century will be found in Appendix B.

The following table, reading from the top manual down, gives a typical order of keyboards and names of the divisions in a four-manual organ.

| United States and England | France |
|---|---|
| IV Solo | IV Bombarde |
| III Swell | III Récit |
| II Great | II Positif |
| I Choir (Positiv) | I Grand Orgue |

| Germany | Holland |
|---|---|
| IV Brustwerk | IV Borstwerk |
| III Oberwerk | III Bovenwerk |
| II Hauptwerk | II Hoofdwerk |
| I Rückpositiv | I Rugwerk |

Couplers, usually in the form of rocking tablets above the upper keyboard, make it possible to play various divisions on keyboards other than their own. The manual divisions may also be coupled to the Pedal division.

The swell (expression) pedal was the outgrowth of the late seventeenth-century practice, especially in Spain, France, and England, of occasionally enclosing one division of the organ in a box in order to produce an echo effect. The actual invention of a box with a shutter, which the organist could open and close by means of a pedal, is usually attributed to the English builder, Abraham Jordan. This crude device, invented in 1712, was gradually improved until the front of the box was provided with a series of shutters resembling a Venetian blind. Various improvements in the operation of the swell pedal were also made. There is no evidence that the swell box, with shutters and a swell pedal, was used in France and Germany until after the time of Bach.

However, Michael Praetorius in the *Organographia* (1619) quotes a burger of Nuremberg who regrets that the organ has a disadvantage in that the organist is not able to give expression to his Affections because the tones of the organ cannot be moderated dynamically and made loud and soft, except by changing stops.

Contemporary organs rarely have more than one or two divisions enclosed (Swell and Choir) and many instruments, like the organs of the Baroque period and before, are entirely unenclosed. The closing of the swell box suppresses the upper partials, and the tones lose much of their character.

The crescendo pedal is a mechanical device for adding or retiring stops progressively. It should be used sparingly, and only when other means of achieving the same results are not possible.

The tremulant is a mechanical device which produces an alternating increase and decrease of wind pressure in the wind trunk which feeds a wind chest.

The tremulant was known early in the sixteenth century, and directions for its use are given by later composers and organ builders. Bach insisted that the tremulant in the organ at his church in Mühlhausen (1708) be "regulated so that it flutters at the proper rate."

The use of the tremulant should be reserved for special effects with appropriate solo stops.

## CLASSES OF PIPES

There are two distinct classes of organ pipes—flue (labial) and reed (lingual).

### Flue Pipes

The tone in a flue pipe is produced by a vibrating column of air within the pipe. The speaking length of the pipe determines its pitch. The flue pipes are tuned by lengthening or shortening the pipe, which is usually done by means of a sliding sleeve on the top of open pipes and by moving the stopper up or down in stopped pipes.

The scale of a pipe is, roughly, the relationship of the diameter to the length. The scale plays an important part in determining the nature of the tone quality of the pipe. Scales are designated as narrow, moderate, and wide.

The tone quality, shape, scale, and material used in stops of the same name will vary considerably with builders of various periods and countries.

### Reed Pipes

Reed pipes use a type of reed known as a beating reed. The tongue (reed) rests on a shallot (brass tube) which is open to the resonator (pipe). When the tongue vibrates, it sets up sympathetic vibrations in the air column within the resonator.

The reed pipes are tuned in two ways: (a) by lengthening or shortening the resonator at its upper end, (b) by adjusting the tuning wire which controls the vibrating length of the tongue.

## QUALITIES OF TONE COLOR

### Flue Pipes

Flue (labial) pipes produce three basic qualities of tone—Principal, Flute, and String.

*Principal Tone* (Principal, Open Diapason, Octave, Quinte, Super Octave, Montre, Prestant, Mixture). This quality is the basic organ tone and is peculiar to the organ.

Principals usually appear at 16′, 8′, 4′, 2⅔′ and 2′ pitches, and are found most completely represented in the Great and Pedal divisions. Principals at various pitches are also found in other divisions, usually at the 4′ pitch in the Swell and at the 2′ pitch in the Positiv, forming the Principal basis for the full ensemble in those divisions.[1]

The Principal pipes are metal, open, and usually cylindrical in shape. In comparison with the flutes, they are narrow in scale and are often classified as "masculine."

*Flute Tone* is divided into the following types: Stopped Flutes, Half-stopped Flutes, Open Flutes, and Harmonic Flutes. Flutes are found at various pitches in all divisions of the organ. The pipes are of wider scale than the Principals and may be made of wood or, more often, of metal. Wood flutes of the Clarabella, Concert Flute, and Melodia type are characteristic of the Romantic organ.

Stopped flutes (Gedackt, Pommer, Bourdon, Nason Flute, Stopped Diapason, Subbass) have large-scale pipes of wood or metal. The pipes have stoppers in the upper end and are half the length of open pipes of the same pitch. Stopped pipes develop the odd-numbered partials (2⅔′, 1⅗′), with strong emphasis on the fundamental pitch (8′). The stopped flutes are useful as a basis for building up various combinations with mutation stops. They may also support Principal stops of higher pitches without using the Principal 8′.

Half-stopped flutes (Rohrflöte, Chimney Flute, Koppelflöte) have a small cylindrical chimney inserted in the stopper, or a cone-shaped extension on the pipe. They have high harmonic development in relation to the fundamental, reinforcing the fifth (1⅗′) and sixth partials (1⅓′).

The Quintadena family of stopped flutes is characterized by having the third partial (2⅔′) developed equally with the fundamental. They are often found at 16′ pitch in the Great and Pedal divisions.

Open flutes have large-scale cylindrical or conical pipes and are often used at the higher pitches. The Hohlflöte, Sifflöte, Holzflöte, and Nachthorn are cylindrical. Conical (tapered) pipes include the Waldflöte, Blockflöte, and Querflöte (overblown).

Harmonic flutes have open pipes of moderate scale which are double the normal length of an open pipe of the same pitch. A small hole just below the center of the pipe helps the pipe to overblow the octave.

Hybrid stops (Gemshorn, Spitzflöte, Erzähler) have conical pipes which form an inverted cone near their top. The second partial (4′) is prominent, and the tone lies somewhat between the flute and string or Principal and flute.

*String Tone* (Gambe, Viola da Gamba, Viole de Gambe, Voix Céleste, Salicional). The string-toned pipes have a high harmonic development and the tone varies from a smooth, broad quality (resembling a quiet Geigen Principal) to a thin, pungent one.

String-toned stops are found principally at unison pitch and are not essential to the basic tonal structure of the organ. The broad type of string combined with the 8′ Gedackt, however, often forms the foundation for a manual chorus. It is also useful as a foundation stop in other types of combinations.

The Céleste is a rank which is tuned a trifle sharp. When combined with another stop of similar quality and intensity, beats are produced which give the effect of a vibrato. The célestes should be sparingly used and never used with a tremulant, or with combinations of several louder stops.

### Reed Pipes

Reed (lingual) pipes produce many different qualities of tone color. They are usually classified according to the type and length of their resonators —Conical, Cylindrical, and Short-length or Fractional (less than half of the normal pitch-length). Within these three groups are chorus reeds, solo reeds, and reeds suitable for both chorus and solo.

1. Conical resonators of approximately normal pitch-length: Trumpet, Posaune, Trombone, Clairon, Bombarde, Kornett, Fagott, Schalmei, Oboe.
2. Cylindrical resonators of half-length: Dulzian, Krummhorn, Zink, Cromorne, Rohrschalmei.
3. Short-length, or fractional resonators: Vox Humana, Regal, Rankett, Sordun, Bärpfeife.

Orchestral reeds include the Orchestral Oboe, Clarinet, Bassoon, English Horn, Heckelphone, Basset Horn, and French Horn. These voices are more or less imitative of the orchestral instrument and are generally most appropriate in music of a romantic character. They are frequently replaced by various combinations of mutation ranks.

A solo Tuba, capable of dominating the full

---

[1] See the "Table of Partials" on page 7.

organ, is frequently found in organs in England and in some in the United States.

The Trompette en Chamade (Clarin) is a brilliant and powerful reed, the pipes of which are projected horizontally and fanwise. It is commonly found in eighteenth-century Spanish organs, and occasionally in English and American organs.

## MUTATION STOPS

The mutation stops correspond to the natural partials of the unison pitch. The various unison partials (8′, 4′, 2′) are considered as foundation stops; the off-unison partials (2⅔′, 1⅗′, 1⅓′, and, rarely, 1⅐′) represent the mutation stops.

The mutation stops are characteristic of the organ, and their principal use is with a unison (8′) or octave (4′) rank to produce a new tone color.

The mutation ranks must be untempered and softer than the unison rank with which they are combined, or the individual ranks will be heard rather than a new and distinctive tone quality.

There are also combinations of several mutation ranks which are usually drawn by one stop-knob and sometimes called mixtures. These include the Sesquialtera, Tertian, and Cornet. They differ from mixtures in that the Tierce is introduced, and there are no breaks in the ranks as the compass only extends to c³.

The Sesquialtera is normally composed of a Nazard (2⅔′) and Tierce (1⅗′). A Larigot (1⅓′) is sometimes added.

The Tertian is composed of a 1⅗′ and a 1⅓′ rank.

The Cornet usually consists of from three to five ranks of mutation stops. The lower ranks are omitted below c¹, and the compass extends to c³. The Cornet has a somewhat reedy tone and may be used as a strong solo voice or combined with reed and flue stops.

A typical Cornet V Rks. would be as follows:

| | |
|---|---|
| C to B | 2⅔′–2′–1⅗′ |
| c to b | 4′–2⅔′–2′–1⅗′ |
| c¹ to c³ | 8′–4′–2⅔′–2′–1⅗′ |

The following table lists the partials and their pitches when found as separate stops. The 8′ series normally appears in the manual divisions, and the 16′ series in the Pedal division. The Septième is rare in organs in the United States, but is frequently found in the larger French organs.

It should be noted that the fundamental pitch (8′) is the first partial and that the second partial (4′) is the first overtone or harmonic. The numbers represent the approximate length of an open pipe at low C.

### Table of Partials

| 8′ Series Partials | | | 16′ Series Partials |
|---|---|---|---|
| First | 8′ | Fundamental | 16′ |
| Second | 4′ | Octave (Prestant) | 8′ |
| Third | 2⅔′ | Twelfth (Quinte) | 5⅓′ |
| Fourth | 2′ | Fifteenth (Super-Octave) | 4′ |
| Fifth | 1⅗′ | Seventeenth (Tierce) | 3⅕′ |
| Sixth | 1⅓′ | Nineteenth (Larigot) | 2⅔′ |
| Seventh | 1⅐′ | Flat twenty-first (Septième) | 2²⁄₇′ |
| Eighth | 1′ | Twenty-second (Sifflöte) | 2′ |

## MIXTURE STOPS

Mixtures are compound stops of from three to six or more ranks of Principal pipes for each note of the keyboard. There are many varieties of mixture stops, but usually the pitches are confined to unison and fifth-sounding ranks.

In organs of the sixteenth and seventeenth centuries, mixtures of 18 or more ranks were not unusual. Praetorius (*Organographia,* 1619) mentioned a mixture of seven pitches and 46–48 ranks. The number of ranks for each pitch varied from two to sixteen.

One of the chief functions of the mixture stops is to give clarity to the ensemble. This is accomplished by breaking back the various ranks at the proper place in the compass, resulting in the lower notes having the higher-pitched ranks and the higher notes having the lower-pitched ranks. Point and definition are thus added to the lower part of the compass, brilliance to the middle part, and breadth and fullness to the upper part. Mixtures also add color, brightness, and intensity to the ensemble.

When the pitch of a mixture is indicated on the stop-knob (2⅔′, 2′, or 1⅓′), it refers to the pitch of the longest C pipe in the mixture.

*Chorus Mixtures* (Mixture, Fourniture, Plein Jeu, Scharf) are composed of unison and fifth-sounding ranks, breaking back one rank at a time.

The following is a typical 2′ Fourniture IV Rks. Mixture.

| | I | II | III | IV |
|---|---|---|---|---|
| C to f | 2′ | –1⅓′ | –1′ | – ⅔′ |
| f♯ to f¹ | 2⅔′ | –2′ | –1⅓′ | –1′ |
| f♯¹ to f² | 4′ | –2⅔′ | –2′ | –1⅓′ |
| f♯² to c⁴ | 8′ | –4′ | –2⅔′ | –2′ |

*Cymbel.* The Cymbel is a high-pitched mixture composed of unison and fifth-sounding ranks, usually breaking at every octave. It adds brilliance to the ensemble and can be used with chorus reeds and the full Principal chorus. One of its special uses is with an 8′ Gedackt in rapid running passages. Sometimes the Cymbel is used for a second mixture of higher pitch than the other mixtures in the same department, in which case the breaks may be more normal. Typical three-rank Cymbels have the following composition: 2′–1⅓′–1′ or 1⅓′–1′–⅔′ or 1′–⅔′–½′.

*Carillon.* This high-pitched mixture is characterized by a somewhat bell-like sound and the inclusion of third-sounding ranks with the octaves and fifths. The mixture may have from two to six ranks, breaking at every octave until the highest pitched ranks which may break at the half octave. Typical three-rank Carillons have the following composition: 2⅔′–1⅗′–1′ or 1′–⅘′–⅔′.

# Registration

The study of registration includes a knowledge of the specifications and tonal characteristics of organs of all periods as well as any registrations suggested by composers, organ builders, or from other sources.

The following brief survey of registrations and organs in Germany, France, Italy, and the United States is intended to form the basis for that study.

## GERMANY

### Seventeenth and Eighteenth Centuries

Samuel Scheidt (1587–1654), a pupil of Sweelinck, gave suggestions for registration in his *Tabulatura Nova* (1624). Scheidt was organist of the Moritzkirche in Halle where he supervised the building of an organ by Heinrich Compenius in 1624 (see Appendix B, No. VIII). Scheidt's registrations are for a two-manual organ and are designed to separate the chorale melody from the other parts by playing it on a separate manual with a clear, penetrating stop or a combination of stops. He also suggested playing an alto chorale melody on the pedal at the proper pitch, leaving the hands free to play the other parts.

Arp Schnitger (1648–1719) in North Germany and Gottfried Silbermann (1683–1753) in Central Germany were the most distinguished and influential organ builders in the middle and late German Baroque.

By the second half of the seventeenth century, the general plan of the north German organ was established. This design, known as the *Werkprinzip*, was followed in Schnitger-type organs. Each division was placed in its own case which was located in a particular place in the instrument. The Principal stops in each division were based on the lowest-pitched Principal rank. Depending on the size of the organ and number of divisions, the Pedal division would be based on a 32′ or 16′ Principal, the *Hauptwerk* a 16′ or 8′, the *Rückpositiv* an 8′ or 4′, and the *Brustwerk* a 2′. Some large organs included an *Oberwerk* as an adjunct to the *Hauptwerk*, and very large organs might have a *Kronwerk* to "crown" the entire organ.

Arp Schnitger built or rebuilt upwards of 150 organs of all sizes, mostly in northwest Germany in the region of Hamburg; a few were built for churches in the Netherlands. The organs followed the *Werkprinzip* arrangement of divisions; each division had its own character and contrasted sharply with the other divisions. The flue and reed choruses were characterized by high harmonic development and variety, and the *Rückpositiv* was unusually brilliant, partly because of its position on the gallery railing at the back of the organist. Mixtures, mutations and reeds were found in all divisions and a preference was often shown for the lower pitches. All divisions, with the possible exception of the *Brustwerk*, included about the same number of stops and complete choruses, especially in the Pedal, as there was no *Hauptwerk* to Pedal coupler.

A typical large Schnitger is represented in his 1688 rebuild of the Hans Scherer organ of 1605 in the *Jacobikirche*, Hamburg (see Appendix B, No. XI).

There are four principal registrations for the late seventeenth-century Schnitger-type organs: *Organo pleno*, Small Ensembles, Solo, and Accompaniment.

1. *Organo pleno* (Principal chorus): Narrow-scale Principals (16′), 8′, 4′, 2⅔′, 2′; Mixtures. Do not use reeds in the *plenum*, draw two stops of the same pitch, or mix Principals and Flutes.
2. *Small Ensembles:* Small choruses of Principals or Flutes on secondary manuals. Occasional use of a Gedackt 8′ as a foundation stop when there is no Principal 8′.
3. *Solo:* Flutes or Principals alone at 8′ pitch or combined with various partials of the same family (4′, 2⅔′, 2′, 1⅓′, 1′), Zimbel, Sesquialtera, Terzian. Combinations of three or more stops of different pitches (8′, 2′, 1′; 16′, 4′, 2′, 1⅓′). Reed stops (Krummhorn, Regal, Schalmei, Dulzian, Vox Humana) used alone or combined

with Principals, rarely Flutes, of higher pitches (4', 2⅔', 1⅓').

4. *Accompaniment:* Principal 8' or Flute 8' alone or with a 4' stop of the same family. The Pedal was unusually complete and effective in pedal solos and as a *cantus firmus*.

The master organ builder of north central Germany during the late Baroque was Gottfried Silbermann (1683–1753). He followed the tradition of his predecessors, among them Casparini, and was also strongly influenced by the sounds of the classical French organ, particularly the *Positif* (Nasard 2⅔', Tierce 1⅗', Quinte 1⅓', Cornet V, Vox Humana, Cromorne (Krummhorn). Eventually Silbermann gave up the *Rückpositiv* in his organs and incorporated the French-type stops into the *Oberwerk* and *Brustpositiv* (see Appendix B, Nos. VI, XVII). The Pedal division varied from only 16' and 8' Principals and reeds to an Untersatz 32' and a Principal chorus and reeds 16', 8', 4'. In small organs the *Hauptwerk* was coupled to the Pedal, but the coupler to Pedal was often omitted in larger instruments.

The following registrations are suggested for the early eighteenth-century Silbermann-type organs.

1. *Organo pleno:* Principals (16'), 8', 4', 2⅔', 2', and mixtures. Principals and flutes of 16', 8', and 4' pitch may be used together, and reeds and stops including the Tierce added to the *plenum.* Lower pitches in manuals and pedal are preferred and manuals might be coupled. The *Oberwerk* (without the Tierce) may be coupled to the *Hauptwerk.*
2. *Small Ensembles:* Various combinations of 16', 8', and 4' flue stops, often with the Sesquialtera (2⅔', 1⅗').
3. *Solos:* Cornet (8', 4', 2⅔', 2', 1⅗'); Gedackt 8, Nasat 2⅔', Tertia (1⅗', 1⅓'); Gedackt, Rohrflöte 4', Nasat 2⅔', Octave 2', Tertia; Gedackt 8', Rohrflöte 4', Sifflot 1'; Skip intervals (8', 2⅔', 1⅗'; 16', 4', 2', 1⅓').
4. *Accompaniment:* Prinzipal 8', Flute 8'; Gedackt 8', Gemshorn 2', Rohrflöte 8', Spitzflöte 4'. The Pedal emphasizes the lower pitches (32', 16', 8').

### Registration of Bach's Organ Works

Carl Philipp Emanuel Bach and Johann Friedrich Agricola, in Bach's *Obituary* (1754), stated that Bach combined the various stops "in the most skillful manner" and displayed each stop "according to its character, in the greatest perfection." C. P. E. Bach also wrote Forkel saying that no one

understood registration as well as his father. He also said "that many organ builders and organists were frightened when they saw him [Bach] pull the stops," but that they "were much surprised when they afterwards perceived that the organ sounded best just so."

Bach played the large organ in the *Katharinenkirche* in Hamburg which had 16' reeds and, according to Jacob Adlung, Bach could not praise the beauty and variety of the tone highly enough. He also admired the 32' pedal Principal and the Trombone.

During his early years Bach had the opportunity of knowing north German organs of the Schnitger-type in Lüneberg, Lübeck, Hamburg and nearby towns. He became acquainted with central German organs when he was engaged to examine and report on new organs in Halle (1714), Erfurt (1716), Leipzig (1717, 1744), and Dresden (1732) where he played Silbermann's organs and expressed his admiration for their "silvery tone and thundering basses."

The organs where Bach was church organist (Arnstadt, 1703–1707 and Mühlhausen, 1708) were relatively small two-manual instruments. At Weimar (1708–1717) he was Court Organist and Chamber Musician, and from 1706 to 1723 Capellmeister at the Calvinist court in Cöthen. His duties at Leipzig (1723–1750), as Cantor and *Director Musices* at the *Thomaskirche,* did not include playing the organ.

In 1708 when Bach was appointed organist at St. Blasius's Church at Mühlhausen, he complained about the defects in the organ and was asked to make recommendations for repair. These are summarized as follows:

New bellows were to be installed, and old windchests rebuilt "so that all stops can be used together."

A new Sub-Bass 32' was to be added with its own windchest, and the Trombone-Bass [Posaune] rebuilt.

The Pedal was also to include a Glockenspiel 4', at the request and expense of the parishioners.

On the *Oberwerk* [*Hauptwerk*] a Fagotto 16' was to replace the Trumpet 8', and a Viol di Gamba the Gemshorn. The Gamba would combine well with the Salicional 4' in the *Rückpositiv.*

A new Nassat 2⅔' was to be installed in the *Hauptwerk* in place of the old Quinta.

A new and "most important matter" was "a new little Brustpositiv" with the following stops. Quinta 3'; Octava 2'; Schalemoy 8'; Mixture, 3 ranks; Tertia, which, with a few other stops, will "produce a fine and complete Sesquialtera"; Fleute douce 4′; Stillgedackt 8′, "which accords perfectly with concerted music." There must be a coupler for the *Brustwerk* to *Hauptwerk,* and "the tremulant must be regulated so that it flutters at the proper rate." (see Appendix B, No. XIV and the *Bach Reader,* pp. 58–60).

Bach's later organ chorales and free compositions (preludes, fugues, toccatas, and some fantasies) are often unified by their style and mood (affect) and should be played on an appropriate *plenum* without a change of manuals. These works, often marked *Organo pleno* (*In, Pro,* or *Cum*), include the Preludes and Fugues in C major (BWV 547), C minor (BWV 546), and B minor (BWV 544), and the Catechism Chorale, *Wir glauben all an einen Gott* (BWV 680).

The use of two manuals is called for in free compositions when there is a change of style and contrasting sections. This change of style is one of the characteristics of the middle-Baroque composers: Bruhns, Lübeck, Buxtehude, and Bach in some of his earlier works (*Prelude and Fugue in D Major,* BWV 532). The change of mood in Bach's *Fantasia in G Minor* (BWV 542), his own indications in the "Dorian" Toccata (BWV 538), the echo passages in the *Prelude in E-flat* (BWV 552), and some concertos also require manual changes. When using two manuals with pedal the subsidiary manual should be strong enough not to require a change of pedal stops.

Registrations for specific stops are indicated in only a few of Bach's organ works. They include the following:

> *Ein' feste Burg* (BWV 720)
> *Gott durch deine Güte* (BWV 600)
> Schübler Chorales (BWV 645–650)
> *Concerto in D Minor* (BWV 596)

Manual indications (*Oberwerk, Hauptwerk* and *Rückpositiv*) are found in the Organ Concertos, *Praeludium* ("Dorian" Toccata BWV 538), *Ein' feste Burg* (BWV 720), *Ach Gott und Herr* (BWV 692), and *Wie schön leuchtet der Morgenstern* (BWV 739).

Organ chorales to be played on two manuals are identified as *à 2 Clav. e Pedale* or *à due Claviere*. In some editions of the *Orgelbüchlein*, BWV 607 and 608 are incorrectly indicated for two manuals, and BWV 633 (*Liebster Jesu*) is omitted.

The utmost care must be used in selecting stops to be used in performing the organ music of Bach, and all other composers, on contemporary organs, especially those of unsuitable design and tonal resources.

Most of the organs of the past centuries have been, or are being rebuilt, mutilated, replaced, or destroyed. A few of the old organs have been carefully restored and may be heard today in their original acoustical setting and on recordings.

The basic principles of registration should be mastered and adapted to the organ on which the music is being performed. With knowledge, imagination, careful listening, and an artistic sensibility, organ music of the Baroque, Romantic and Contemporary eras can be effectively performed on widely diverse organs.

## FRANCE

### Seventeenth and Eighteenth Centuries

From the middle of the seventeenth century until the late eighteenth century the design of the French organ evolved into its classic form. Although the concept of this design varied among builders and registrations of the time reflected some individual differences in taste, the similarity of instruments and registrations is readily apparent.

The main divisions of the organ were the *Grand Orgue* and the *Positif,* which in its tonal design was a smaller reflection of the *Grand Orgue* and was coupled to it in ensemble combinations. On larger organs the divisions called the *Récit, Echo* and *Bombarde* were much smaller and limited in compass. The *Pédale* division was also very small, generally including a *Flûte* 8′ and 4′ and also, on larger organs, a *Trompette* 8′. The *Grand Orgue* and *Positif* were coupled together in ensemble combinations, and the *Grand Orgue* was often coupled to the *Pédale.*

In spite of the fact that ensemble and solo combinations followed prescribed patterns the reeds, colorful mutation stops, and particularly the characteristic *Cornet* sound, gave great variety and character to the music.

The following registrations by Dom Bédos, Le Bègue, Nivers, and Raison are taken from the original sources.

*Ensemble*

Dom Bédos (1770)
1. *Plein Jeu*
   Grand Orgue and Positif: all Montres [16′, 8′], Bourdons [16′, 8′], Open Flutes [8′], Prestants [4′], Doublettes [2′], Fournitures, Cymbales. Keyboards coupled.
   Pédale: Trompette(s) [8′], Clairon(s) [4′]. Flutes may be used in the Pedal division in

place of the reeds, especially when there is a 16′ flute. However, flutes should not be combined with the pedal reeds.

2. *Grand Jeu*

Grand Orgue: Grand Cornet, Prestant, all the Trompettes and the Clairons.

Positif: Cornet, Prestant, Trompette, Clairon, Cromorne (the Cromorne is omitted if the Grand Orgue has only one Trompette and one Clairon). Keyboards coupled. Do not use the Tremulant.

Récit: Cornet.

Echo: Cornet.

Pédale: Trompette (s) , Clairon (s) .

## Fugue

Guillaume–Gabriel Nivers (1665)

1. *Fugue Grave*
   a. Gros jeu de Tierce with Tremulant.
   b. Trompette without the Tremulant.

Nicolas Le Bègue (1676)

1. *Fugue Grave*
   a. Grand Orgue: Bourdon, Prestant, Trompette, Clairon.
   b. On small organs: Bourdon, Cromhorne.

Dom Bédos (1770)

1. *Fugue de Mouvement*
   a. Grand Jeu.
   b. Grand Orgue: Grand Jeu de Tierce.
      Positif: Jeu de Tierce.
      Keyboards coupled.

## Duo

Guillaume–Gabriel Nivers (1665)

1. Treble: Petite Tierce [Bourdon 8′, Prestant, Nazard, Tierce].
   Bass: Grosse Tierce [Bourdon 16′, Montre 8′, Bourdon 8′, Prestant, Nazard, Doublette, Tierce].
2. Treble: Cornet.
   Bass: Trompette.

## Trio

André Raison (1714)

1. Treble: (two parts on one keyboard) Positif: Cromorne
   Bass: Grand Orgue: Bourdon [8′], Prestant [4′], Flûte [8′], Nazard, Tierce, Tremblant doux [a tremulant enclosed in the wind trunk].
2. Treble: Positif: Bourdon [8′], Flûte [4′], Nazard, Tremblant doux.
   Bass: Grand Orgue: Bourdon [8′], Flûte [8′].

*Solo and Accompaniment*

Nicolas Le Bègue (1676)

1. *Tierce en Taille* [Récit de Tierce en Taille].
   Grand Orgue [accompaniment]: Montre 16′ or Bourdon 16′, Bourdon [8′], Prestant; or, Montre [8′], Bourdon [8′]; or Montre [8′], Bourdon [8′], Prestant; or Bourdon [8′], Prestant.
   Positif: Montre [8′], Bourdon [8′] Flûte [4′], Nazard, Doublette, Tierce, Larigot.
   Pédale: [Flûte].
2. *Cromorne en Taille*
   Grand Orgue: Same as the Tierce en Taille.
   Positif: Montre [8′], Bourdon [8′], Nazard, Cromorne.

# ITALY

### Seventeenth Century

The tonal design of the classic Italian organ was established during the early Baroque and remained constant for many years. Because of this, the music of Girolamo Frescobaldi (1583–1643) may be suitably registered according to suggestions by Constanzo Antegnati (1608) and Adriano Banchieri (1611). Although two-manual instruments existed at the time of Frescobaldi, the typical organ had only one manual with a compass of four octaves, the first octave being "short." In larger organs the manual compass was extended lower and the manual was permanently coupled to the Pedal. The longest Pedal compass was two octaves, one a "short" octave, the other a full chromatic one. Occasionally a 16′ stop, the Contrabassi, was included as an independent pedal rank. Some organs had divided stops, and Antegnati mentioned the use of such a stop in his registration instructions.

The Principal *plenum*, called the *ripieno*, was the essential feature of the Italian organ, and its tonal quality was characterized by clarity and brilliance without aggressiveness. This family of Principals was composed of independent unison and fifth-sounding ranks which were named according to their pitch relation to the fundamental Principal (8′ or 16′) (see Specifications IV and V, Appendix B). There were no mixture stops. The independent stops of the Principal family were combined in many ways to give great variety to the sound of the organ. In addition to the Principals there were two or three ranks of flutes which were never included in the *ripieno* but were added individually to the Principal to create new color. Reeds were rare, the most common one being the Regal. The Fiffaro, or Voce umana, was a Principal rank beginning at tenor g or c¹ and tuned "in beats" with the Principal 8' to create a vibrato effect. A tremulant was mentioned in some registrations.

In registering Italian music on a contemporary organ, use stops that give clarity and brightness to the ensemble; avoid aggressive, thick sounds. A bright open flute would be preferable to a heavy Principal as a foundation tone. A *ripieno* based on the 8' Principal does not include the 2⅔' pitch. The use of mixtures should be avoided, since the mixture ranks break back throughout the compass, and the individual ranks of the Italian organ broke back only in the higher registers. In pieces where a pedal part might be appropriate, balance the manual combination with a light 16' flue stop.

Costanzo Antegnati (1549–1624), a member of a well-known family of organ builders and organists, published his L'Arte Organica in Brescia in 1608. The following suggestions are taken from this important treatise on organ building and the art of registration.

1. *Ripieno:* The chorus of Principal stops. For pieces such as *Intonations* or the *Toccata* preceding a Mass.
2. *Mezzo ripieno:* Principal 8', Octave 4', Twenty-ninth ½', Thirty-third ⅓', Octave Flute 4'. Also the Principal 8', Octave 4', Twenty-second 1', Twenty-sixth ⅔', Octave Flute 4'.
3. *Concerto di cornetti:* Octave 8', Nineteenth 2⅔', Twenty-second 2', Octave Flute 8'.
4. For the *Elevation:* Principal 8' alone or with the *Voce umana.*
5. For *Canzoni alla francese:* Principal 8' and Flute 4'. Also other combinations of stops.

Antegnati suggested changing registrations, when suitable, during the course of the music.

# GERMANY

### *Nineteenth Century*

In Germany the "simplified" organ of J. G. Vogler (1748–1814), who was called a "musical buffoon" by Mozart but admired by others, gave way to a renaissance in organ building led by E. F. Walcker (1794–1872). The organs built by Walcker and others, beginning in the third decade of the nineteenth century, were often large instruments. They included complete ensembles, sometimes with two Principal choruses, low-pitched mixtures, chorus reeds, and a considerable number of stops of 8' pitch. There were Cornets and mutations but few, if any, solo reeds or célestes. Often one division was

in a swell box and a crescendo pedal was included.

The builders of these organs, as the specifications indicate, made no attempt to imitate the orchestra, and the instruments were well suited to the music of the relatively few outstanding German composers for organ of the nineteenth century. Although many of the organs included mechanical accessories associated with the so-called "romantic" organ, the builders did not begin to abandon tradition until the last two decades of the century.

There are comparatively few directions for the use of specific stops in the organ music of Mendelssohn, Schumann, Liszt, Brahms, Rheinberger, or Reger. The general principle of registration in nineteenth-century Germany was stated by Mendelssohn in the Preface to his *Six Sonatas*. Because of the difference in organs he gave "only a general indication of the kind of effect intended to be produced, without giving a precise List of the particular Stops to be used."

Mendelssohn continued with the "Prefatory Remarks" in the original edition of his Sonatas: "By 'Fortissimo', I intend to designate the Full Organ: by 'Pianissimo', I generally mean a soft 8 feet Stop alone: by 'Forte', the Great Organ, but without some of the most powerful stops: by 'Piano', some of the soft 8 feet Stops combined: and so forth. . . . In the Pedal part, I should prefer throughout, even in the Pianissimo passages the 8 feet & the 16 feet Stops united: except when the contrary is expressly specified (see the 6th Sonata) . . ." There is little doubt that the musician Mendelssohn elaborated on these simple indications.

The dynamic marks also indicated the manual to be used (I, ff or f; II, mf or p; III, pp). These were sometimes supplemented by qualifying words ("dolce" by Brahms indicating a reduction in volume), tempo marks, and rarely some suggestions for interpretation.

The registration for Reubke's *Ninety-fourth Psalm* was indicated in the original edition by his brother Otto. The first performance of both Reubke's work and Liszt's *Ad nos, ad salutarem undam,* and *Prelude and Fugue on B A C H* took place in Merseburg Cathedral in 1855 on a large organ rebuilt by the north-central German builder Friedrich Ladegast. This famous organ included stops of wide dynamic range, from an Unda Maris to powerful principals and reeds (see *The Organ* by W. L. Sumner, p. 484).

A four-manual Walcker organ, opened in the Boston Music Hall in 1863, included upwards of 90 stops, an enclosed Swell division, a crescendo pedal, and a number of reversible combination pedals. Unusual features were a two-rank Vox Humana and the separation of the Pedal into "forte" and "piano" divisions, the latter enclosed in a swell box. This organ exerted considerable influence on builders in the United States, and many fine organs were built during the following years (see *The History of the Organ in the United States* by Orpha Ochse, pp. 199–205).

## FRANCE

### Nineteenth Century

Organ building in the 18th century reached a high level with the instruments of Henri Cliquot (1728–1790), among them the great organ in Saint-Sulpice, Paris (1781), built under the direction of Dom Bédos.

Aristide Cavaillé-Coll (1811–1899) superseded Cliquot and became the most famous builder in nineteenth-century France. One of his aims was to make the new "symphonic" organ more expressive, and his emphasis on 8' tone, new types of flute stops, and brilliant reeds justified César Franck's remark: "Mon nouvel orgue? c'est un orchestre."

The Cavaillé-Coll organs were, with minor exceptions, remarkably uniform in design. However, there is a marked difference in the design and control of Cavaillé-Coll organs compared with those in other countries, and these differences must be understood before registering music by French composers.

The organ works of César Franck (1822–1890), Charles-Marie Widor (1844–1937), Louis Vierne (1870–1937), and other French composers were generally registered for the instruments with which they were associated. A few of the typical features of the Cavaillé-Coll organs and registrations are as follows:

The stop combinations are controlled by ventils (*appels*) which are operated by locking pedals. The ventils control the admission of the air to various wind chests so that the stops can be drawn (with the ventil pedal released) but will not sound until the pedal belonging to that particular chest is depressed. Thus *Anches préparées* indicates that the reeds are to be drawn (prepared) and added when desired by operating the ventil pedal.

The *Récit* (Swell) is the only enclosed division. Dynamic indications for the *Récit,* or for another manual to which the *Récit* is coupled, refer to the position of the *Récit* expression pedal and not to the loudness of the stops. Thus the indication "pp," when playing on the *Récit* with all stops drawn, would mean that the box is to be closed. The indication "f," when playing on the Voix Céleste, would

mean that the box is to be open. Dynamic indications for the unenclosed divisions refer to the volume of tone required.

The foundation stops (*Fonds*) include the flue stops of 32', 16', 8', 4', 2' pitch as opposed to the mixtures, mutations, and reeds.

Stops of the same pitch are often drawn together, particularly the Harmonic Flute 8' and the Bourdon 8'.

The French reeds, with or without mixtures, are used to give power and brilliance to the ensemble.

The organ in Sainte-Clotilde, for which Franck registered his organ compositions, was different in several respects from the typical Cavaillé-Coll organ.

1.  The Trompette on the *Récit* was comparatively mild, and Franck often added 8' foundation stops to increase the volume.
2.  The Clarinette was in the unenclosed Positif division, and Franck for that reason often specified the Trompette in the *Récit* for expressive melodies. The Clarinette was later moved to the *Récit* division.
3.  The full *Récit* was somewhat lacking in power and brilliance, and Franck often found it necessary to increase the volume by playing on the *Positif* with the *Récit* coupled.
4.  The Salicional resembled a quiet Geigen Principal and was totally unlike the Salicional found in most organs in the United States (see Appendix B, No. X).

## UNITED STATES

### Twentieth Century

The early decades of the century saw the "orchestral" organ (represented by Ernest M. Skinner and others) at its height in the United States. Organ building in Europe was relatively unaffected by this movement, although there was some decrease in the number of mixtures and an increase in the number of solo reeds.

The organs in the United States during this period emphasized orchestral solo effects, extreme variations in volume, strong color contrasts, large-scale Diapasons, and solo Tubas. Occasionally all divisions, including the Great and Pedal, were enclosed.

Mixtures and mutations were almost nonexistent. The ensemble was neglected, and many smaller organs were built with only 8' and 4' stops on the manuals and a meager Pedal. Unification and the duplexing of stops were common practices, and some of the Pedal divisions had few, if any, independent stops.

In the early 1900s Albert Schweitzer began to question the "romantic" design of some late nineteenth-century organs in Europe, but it was not until about 1920 that the German builders began to turn toward a neo-Baroque style, the so-called "Organ Reform Movement."

Since about 1930 there have been new and important developments in organ design and building in the United States. G. Donald Harrison and Walter Holtkamp pioneered the "American Classic Organ" in the early 1930's, and the electronic organ was born about the same time.

The stated purpose of the Classic Organ was to revive the best qualities of the Baroque organ and retain some of the characteristics of the orchestral organ, including electro-pneumatic action.

The Classic Organ is characterized by unenclosed divisions (Pedal, Great, Positiv), low wind pressures, clarity and transparency of tone, properly voiced mutation and mixture ranks, emphasis on ensemble, and an independent Pedal. To this basic instrument is often added a brilliant reed chorus in the "French" style, other types of solo or ensemble reeds, an enclosed division (Swell), and céleste ranks.

Mechanical (tracker) action organs began to be built in the late 1930's. After World War II there was a rapid development of this type of organ, partly the result of the importation of organs from Germany, Holland, Austria, and Canada. Since the 1960's many fine mechanical action organs have been built in the United States.

The principal characteristics of the mechanical action organ include slider chests, an instrument of moderate size with each division founded on a Principal of 16′, 8′, 4′, or 2′ pitch, low-wind pressures, open toe-holes, and little or no nicking. When possible, each division is placed in a case with display pipes, often of great beauty.

Registration on the large number of diverse organs in the United States requires a comprehensive knowledge of everything related to the subject. Organ music cannot be registered just by the names of the stops; their sound and usefulness will vary with every organ and every acoustical environment. The organist must strive, by careful listening, to realize the intentions of the composer and the essential qualities of the music through the choice of appropriate stops and their combination. It is also important to consider the relationship of the music to the organ on which it is to be performed.

The following basic principles will be of help to the student in the study of registration, particularly for an organ that is well designed, well voiced, and well placed. Inadequate instruments will often make it necessary to modify or alter some of these principles in order to achieve a reasonably satisfactory sound.

1. Avoid unnecessarily complicated registrations. Make changes when the music demands it.
2. Use as few stops as possible. Loudness of tone is not proportional to the number of pipes speaking.
3. Combinations of stops should usually speak at different pitches.
4. To increase the apparent loudness of a tone, increase the intensity of the upper partials by adding them in their normal order.
5. Do not duplicate stops of the same pitch without good reason. Color the stop by the addition of one or more upper partials.
6. Let the registration grow out of the structure and inner content (affect) of the music.
7. Explore the beauty of individual stops.
8. Use the manuals uncoupled whenever possible. Use manual to Pedal couplers, in general, only in ensemble combinations when the Pedal does not have an independent melodic line.
9. Avoid the use of 16′ and 4′ couplers and excessive use of the swell pedal.
10. Leave all soft stops, célestes, tremulants, and color stops (vox humana, orchestral oboe, clarinet) out of full combinations. Use only stops which contribute to the ensemble.

*part two*

# Performance Practice

# Ornamentation

Ornamentation has been a part of Western music since the early development of Gregorian chant. It began as a spontaneous elaboration of a melody, and eventually some of these ornamentations were written into the music or indicated by special signs.

Some signs indicating ornamentation appeared as early as the fifteenth century, and signs are prevalent in English music of the sixteenth century. The technique of improvised ornamentation was much more generally used in the sixteenth century and was described by a number of theorists and practiced by famous organists of the time. Among these were Cabezón, Merulo, Diruta, and Sancta Maria. The signs, which represent the shape of the ornaments more or less pictorially, were systematized by the French composers during the seventeenth century. These composers included a table of ornaments (agréments) in their organ and clavecin books; one of the most comprehensive of these tables was published in 1689 by J. H. d'Anglebert. His table of ornaments and that of François Couperin (1713) exerted a strong influence on other composers in France and Germany, particularly J. S. Bach.

A table of ornaments, however, can only serve as a guide to the melodic shape of the ornament. It does not indicate the many possible variations in the treatment of the dissonant notes, the speed and number of repercussions in trills, and other interpretive factors.

The ability to play ornaments well is indispensable to the musician and should not be taken lightly. Ornaments are not only an integral part of the melodic line, but they affect the rhythm, harmony, structure, and all the details of a musicianly performance.

A study of the sixteenth-, seventeenth-, and eighteenth-century sources which deal with ornamentation, and the modern writings on the subject, reveal that there are many conflicting opinions regarding the performance of certain ornaments. There are, however, many basic principles which emerge and on which authorities are in general agreement. With increased knowledge and the development of good taste and musical understanding, the problems can be solved with confidence.

A musical performance of all music, but especially that of the Renaissance and Baroque, requires a high degree of knowledge and technique, the proper instrument, and above all, sound musicianship. The student should not be so intent on following the so-called "rules" that an unmusical performance results under the guise of "authenticity."

The following section will survey the principles of ornamentation as given by Bach and a few of his predecessors in Italy, England, France, and Germany. It should be pointed out that the examples of ornamentation which follow must be thoroughly understood and mastered before attempting to make exceptions. The organist will gradually develop a personal style and recreate the composer's intentions, as Couperin said, "according to his good taste and fine judgment."

## ITALY

### Girolamo Diruta (1557–1612)

*Il Transilvano* (1593) [1]

Diruta's *tremoli* (trills) begin on the main note, which alternates with the upper auxiliary. They take only half the value of the note, and they are sometimes played slowly and other times quickly.

*Tremoletti* (half trills) include the rapid short trill (main note and upper auxiliary) and the double mordent (main note and lower auxiliary).

[1] *Il Transilvano: Dialogo sopra il vero modo di sonar organi, et istromenti da penna* (Venice: Giacoma Vincenti, 1593). (The Transylvanian: Dialogue on the true method of playing the organ and quilled instruments), I: 10.

## The Gabrielis

Andrea Gabrieli (c. 1515–1586) and Giovanni Gabrieli (1557–1612) wrote out ornamentation in their music. The examples are typical cadential ornaments.

### Girolamo Frescobaldi (1583–1643)

Frescobaldi's ornaments consisted principally of diminutions (groups of short notes in place of a long note), trills, mordents, and turns. The ornaments were written out, except for the few trills which were indicated by the letters t or tr. These trills follow, in general, the pattern of the written-out trills and begin on the main (written) note.

In the Preface to his *Toccate* (1614/16) Frescobaldi states:

. . . the last notes of trills, passages by leaps and steps, must be held longer, even if they be eighths or sixteenths, and dissimilar to those which follow: this pause will avoid confusing the passage with another.

From the *Fiori Musicali* (1635) :

In the *Toccate* when a trill or a tender passage occurs it should be played more slowly.

The following examples are from the *Fiori Musicali:*

## ENGLAND

English ornaments in the seventeenth century were performed in much the same way as those in France and Germany and follow the almost universal custom of beginning on the beat and not before the beat. However, the names of the ornaments and their symbols were different.

### Henry Purcell (1659–1695)

Henry Purcell gives the following "Rules for Graces" in his *Choice Collection of Lessons* (pub. 1696) :

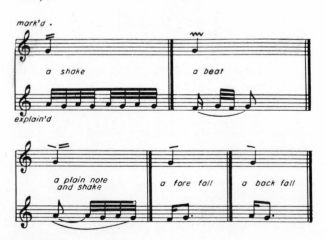

*the turn*     *the shake turn'd*     *a slur*

Purcell also gives a written explanation of the signs. The *shake* (trill) always begins with the note above the main note. The *beat* (appoggiatura from below and mordent) begins a whole step or a half step below the main note, according to the key. The use of the trill sign for this ornament is unique with English composers. In the *plain note and shake* (appoggiatura from above and short trill), the appoggiatura (plain note) is held for about half the value of the main note if it is even, and two-thirds the value of the main note if it is dotted.

### George Frideric Handel (1685–1759)

Ornamentation in the organ works of Handel was sometimes written out, and he used comparatively few signs. The addition of appropriate ornaments, especially in slow movements and at cadences, was undoubtedly the practice of his time. Trills should almost invariably begin on the upper auxiliary, but there are occasions when they may begin on the main note "in the Italian manner."

# FRANCE

### Nicolas Antoine Le Bègue (1630–1702)

Le Bègue included the following ornaments, plus the *Pincé*, in the table in his *Livre d'Orgue* (1676):

*Cadence ou tremblement*     *Harpègement*     *Coulé*

### Jean Henri d'Anglebert (1628–1691)

The table of ornaments of d'Anglebert, given in his *Pièces de Clavecin* (1689), represents the art of French ornamentation at its height. The tables of G.-G. Nivers (1632–1714), Gaspard Corette (c.

1680–c. 1712), and André Raison (c. 1640–1719), although not so complete, follow most of the same principles.

The following "Marques des Agréments et leur Signification" were taken from d'Anglebert's table. *Cheute* was his name for appoggiatura. *Pincé* was the common French term for mordent.

*Tremblement simple*     *Tremblement appuyé*

*Cadence*     *autre*

*Double cadence*     *Sans tremblement*

*Coulé sur tierce*     *Autre*     *Arpégé*     *Autre*

*Cheute ou port de voix en montant*     *En descendant*     *Cheute sur une note*

### François Couperin (1668–1733)

Couperin's table of ornaments was published in his *Pièces de Clavecin* (1713) and explained in *L'Art de Toucher le Clavecin* (1717). His interpretation of the ornaments follows closely that of d'Anglebert. It will be observed that Couperin's examples are notated so that they appear to anticipate the beat. According to his written instructions, however, the ornaments begin on the beat as was customary.

The following "Explication des Agréments et des Signes de Couperin" was taken from his *Pièces de Clavecin* (1713).

Couperin gives the following explanations in his *L'Art de toucher le Clavecin* (1717):

"It is the value of the notes which must determine the duration of the graces such as *Pincés doubles* [long mordents]; *Ports-de-voix-doubles* [appoggiatura from below followed by a long mordent]; and *Tremblements* [trills].

"The repercussions [notes of the trill], and the note on which one stops must all be included in the value of the main note.

"Although trills are indicated by notes of equal value in the "Table of Graces" in my first book, they must nevertheless begin more slowly than they end: but this gradation should be imperceptible.

On whatsoever note a trill may be marked, it must always begin on the tone or semitone above.

"Trills of any considerable duration consist of three parts, which in the execution appear as one and the same thing: 1) Sustaining or dwelling [*l'appuy*] on the note above the main note; 2) the repercussions; 3) the stop [*point d'arrêt*]."

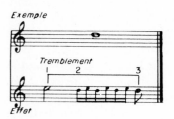

### *Louis-Claude d'Aquin (1694–1772)*

The principal ornaments used by d'Aquin are illustrated in the following table. The sign (+) was also used for the mordent (AₙV).

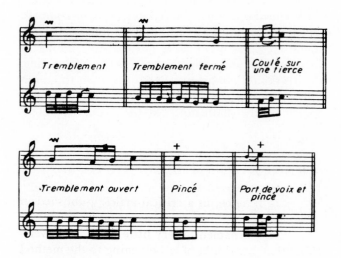

# GERMANY

### *Dietrich Buxtehude (1637–1707)*

The influence of Frescobaldi is evident in the ornamentation which is found in Buxtehude's music (*Te Deum laudamus*, meas. 159). When the trill sign is over a consonant note, the trill may begin with the upper auxiliary. When the trill sign is over a dissonant note, then the trill may begin on the principal note.

### *Georg Muffat (1653–1704)*

Georg Muffat studied with Lully in Paris for six years and with Corelli in Rome (1681–82). Muffat's ornaments show the influence of the French style, and in his *Apparatus musico-organisticus* (1690) he gives an explanation, in Latin, of the abbreviations *P.M.* (pedals *ad libitum*) ; *P.S.* (pedals only) ; *M.S.* (manuals only) . He also gives written directions for the performance of four types of trills, realized in the following examples.

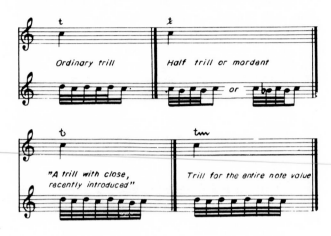

### J. S. Bach (1685–1750)

Bach was strongly influenced by the French style of ornamentation and, to some extent, by the Italian style. He followed the French composers, d'Anglebert in particular, in the signs he used for ornaments and in their interpretation. He frequently wrote out melodic figurations in Italian style and turns, mordents, appoggiaturas, and trills in the French manner.

J. A. Scheibe, in a critical article published in 1737,[2] wrote:

"Every ornament, every little grace, and everything that one thinks of as belonging to the method of playing, he [Bach] expresses completely in notes; and this not only takes away from his pieces the beauty of harmony but completely covers the melody throughout."

Bach included a table of ornaments in the *Clavier-Büchlein* which he began in 1720 for the musical instruction of his nine-year-old son, Wilhelm Friedemann. This table includes thirteen frequently used ornaments, but it does not include all the ornaments used by Bach (see page 27) .

In order to illustrate the use of the ornaments in a composition, Bach followed his table of ornaments by an *Applicatio* bearing the inscription *In Nomine Jesu* (In the Name of Jesus) . The fingering is of special interest, and is one of only two

2 H. T. David and A. Mendel, eds., *The Bach Reader.* (New York: W. W. Norton, 1966) , p. 238.

known examples of pieces fingered by Bach (see page 28) .

Some of the basic principles in the interpretation of ornaments in the organ works of Bach are enumerated below. It should be remembered that musical considerations come before rules, that there are always exceptions, and that more than one interpretation of an ornament may be possible. Context and certain harmonic considerations, such as parallel fifths and octaves, will make some adjustments necessary.

Bach's intentions are not always clear in his manuscripts or in works published in his lifetime. Modern editions of his works are not always reliable, as signs are sometimes omitted, placed over the wrong notes, or misinterpreted.

The student will do well, however, to follow at first the basic principles given below and continue to develop his scholarship and musical judgment to a point where he can play ornaments with musical taste and due regard for their historical background.

1. The primary function of ornaments is an **expressive** one.
2. Ornaments are as much a part of the music as the written notes.
3. The first note of every ornament, with **one** possible exception, begins on the beat (see "The Appoggiatura," p. 25) .
4. The dissonant note or notes receive emphasis, especially in expressive music.
5. Ornaments should be played in the key in which the passage is written, but not necessarily in the key of the composition.

In the following examples, the ornaments as given by Bach in his table are identified by his name.

### The Trill (trillo, tremblement, shake, cadence)

Bach used the following signs to represent a trill, either short or long:ᴡ, ᴍᴍ,t,tr,tᴍᴍ,+.

The number and speed of the repercussions will be determined by the length of the trilled note and by the tempo and character of the music. Excessive speed should always be avoided.

The trill sign is invariably placed over a harmony note, and the trill should begin with the upper auxiliary, which is a dissonance and, as such, receives the stress.

The student may find it helpful at first to measure the repercussions and practice all trills in notes that are half the value of the shortest accompanying notes.

# APPLICATIO FROM J. S. BACH'S

*Clavier-Büchlein vor Wilhelm Friedemann Bach (1720)*

### 1. *Il Transilvano* (1609) [4]        Girolamo Diruta (1557–1612)

The above example shows different kinds of *groppi* at the cadence.

### 2. *Arte de tañer Fantasia* (1565) [5]        Tomás de Sancta Maria (c. 1515–1570)

The above examples show *glosas* on various intervals.

Books by Brown, Donington, and Ferguson, and an article by Horsely dealing with the subject of sixteenth-century embellishment are listed in Appendix **D**. A modern embellishment of a sixteenth-century *clausula* with *glosas* may be found on page 99.

---

4 *Il Transilvano* (1609), Part II, Book I, p. 13.

5 *Libro llamado Arte de tañer Fantasia assi para Tecla como para Vihuela* (Book called the art of playing a fantasia on the keyboard as well as on the vihuela (Valladolid, 1565), I:68v. Otto Kinkeldey, *Orgel und Klavier in der Musik des 16. Jahrhunderts* (Leipzig, 1910), pp. 48, 49.

The following facsimile of one page from Girolamo Diruta's *Il Transilvano* shows the original four-part *Canzona* by Antonio Mortare intabulated with diminutions by Diruta.[6] In the transcription on page 33 the four-part score has been reduced to modern keyboard notation.

6 *Il Transilvano* (1609), Part II, Book I, p. 18.

## 3b. *Canzona, "l'Albergona," Antonio Mortaro (intabulated with diminutions by Girolamo Diruta)*

The letters in the score refer to ornaments and diminutions, as follows: C = *Clamatione*—M = *Minuta*—G = *Groppo*—T = *Tremolo*—A = *Accento*

# Notes Inégales

*"We write differently from the way we play. . . . For example we dot several eighth notes in succession moving by conjunct degrees; however, we write them in equal time values."*[7]

François Couperin

The convention of playing *notes inégales* (unequal notes) has been known since the sixteenth century. However, most of the information comes from treatises written by French musicians in the seventeenth and eighteenth centuries, and these writers are in general agreement.

An understanding of the appropriate use of *notes inégales* is essential to the performance of organ music by French composers of that period. Most of the following information is taken from treatises by Michel de Saint-Lambert and Étienne Loulié.

### The Use of Inequality

1. The purpose of using *notes inégales* is to give elegance (*grâce*) to the line.
2. The character of a piece, its tempo, and the prevailing note values help to determine which notes are made unequal and how much inequality should be used. One pattern of inequality is not necessarily maintained throughout a piece.
3. Inequality usually applies to pairs of notes in conjunct motion.
4. Inequality between two notes of an evenly written pair may vary from a slight lengthening to the considerable lengthening of the first note. It should be understood that time values in examples of *notes inégales* can only be approximate. However, the unequal pair must fill the time value of the equal pair.

Examples:

5. Pairs of dotted notes ( ♩. ♪, ♫ etc.) are played ( ♩.. ♪, ♫ etc.)
6. Inequality is applied to the subdivisions of the basic time unit of the measure. However, if there are many notes of shorter value than these subdivisions they in turn become unequal and the subdivisions remain equal. For example, in a piece with a time signature of 3/2 the half note is the basic time unit. The subdivisions of the half notes, the quarters, would be treated with inequality. However, if there were more eighth notes than quarters in the piece, the eighths would receive the inequality and the quarters would be equal.

### Inequality Is Not Used

1. In pieces marked *detaché, marqué, notes égales.*
2. In the accompaniment. However, imitative phrases in the accompaniment are sometimes played with inequality at the performer's discretion.

    Example: F. Couperin, *Messe pour les Paroisses: Kyrie,* 3e couplet, *Récit de Chromhorne.*
3. When a dot or short vertical line over the notes indicates detached playing.
4. In melodies with disjunct intervals, many syncopations, rests, skips, or mixed note values.
5. In pieces of unsuitable character, such as fugal movements or straightforward pieces.

    Example: F. Couperin, *Petitte fugue sur le Chromhorne* (see page 107).

It is important to remember that the use of *notes inégales* is only a part of the French style. The patterns must enhance the musical line and not call attention to themselves through exaggerated use. The advice of the French musicians to use good taste (*bon goût*) must be carefully heeded.

A thorough study of the convention of *notes inégales* is essential to a convincing performance. Detailed information on the subject may be found in books by Borrel, Couperin, Donington, Ferguson, Harich-Schneider, Loulié, Mellers, and Saint-Lambert and periodical articles by Borrel, Donington, Neumann in Appendix D.

---

[7] *The Art of Playing the Harpsichord*, ed. and trans. by Margery Halford (New York: Alfred Publishing Co., 1974), p. 49.

# Fingering

*"In a succession of notes always watch to see what follows and choose a fingering which will make the progression smooth and easy. Develop equal facility with all five fingers."*[8]

Juan Bermudo

This section includes examples of fingering from the first preserved fingering in Hans Buchner's *Fundamentum* (c. 1520) to C.P.E. Bach's *Essay on the True Art of Playing Keyboard Instruments* (1753).

The importance of fingering in playing keyboard instruments has been recognized throughout the centuries and developed to meet the requirements of the music. However, it was not until the late eighteenth century that keyboard fingering became more or less standardized.

The subject of early fingering was brought to the attention of keyboardists in modern times through the pioneering books of Otto Kinkeldey and Arnold Dolmetsch in the early twentieth century and by the many books, articles, and facsimiles of early treatises published since that time. The knowledge and, above all, the understanding and use of some of the principles of early fingerings are aids in determining the articulation, phrasing, and rhythm for the performance of Renaissance and Baroque organ music.

The early fingerings were used in playing all keyboard instruments. These included the clavichord, harpsichord, virginals, and the regal, portative, positive, and some larger organs. These early instruments generally had relatively short keys and a shallow key fall which favored the fingering. Also, much of the early music was modal and was played principally on the white keys.

Articulations were produced by using the same finger on consecutive notes. The fingers might also be paired, or in groups of three or four notes, and the entire hand moved to the next position.

The technique of turning the thumb under the fingers or passing the fingers over the thumb is not clearly defined in the original sources. However, Luys Venégas de Henestrosa, in a collection of music he edited and published in 1657, gives a number of scale fingerings and specifically directs the player to pass the third finger over the thumb.

There are numerous examples of the fingering, 2–1, in the left hand ascending, and Sancta Maria in his *Arte de tañer Fantasia* (1565) states that the second finger is raised higher than the thumb each time it has struck a note, while the thumb "appears to drag over the keys."

Substitution was not a part of early finger techniques, although Correa de Arauxo gives an example in his *Facultad Orgánica* (1626). Chordal passages were played in a slightly detached manner.

A few general principles of fingering in the 16th and 17th centuries follow[9]:

1.  The three middle fingers (2,3,4) were used the most, the thumb occasionally, and the fifth finger rarely.
2.  The second and fourth fingers were considered "good" fingers and were often placed on rhythmically strong ("good") notes. In the seventeenth century the 1st and 3rd fingers were often considered "good" and the rules ignored.
3.  In right-hand passages the 3rd finger was passed over the 4th in ascending (2,3–4,3–4) and over the 2nd in descending (4,3–2,3–2).
4.  In left-hand passages, the 3rd finger was passed over the 2nd in ascending (4,3–2,3–2) and over the 4th in descending (2,3–4).
5.  The thumb was used in the right hand but more frequently in the left, especially in the progression 2–1,2–1 ascending. Here the second finger may pass over the thumb.
6.  Octaves were fingered $\frac{5}{1}$; fifths and sixths $\frac{4}{1}$ or $\frac{5}{2}$; thirds $\frac{2}{1}$, $\frac{3}{1}$, or $\frac{4}{2}$.

[8] *Declaración de instrumentos musicales* (Osuna, 1555) (Treatise concerning musical instruments). Otto Kinkeldey, *Orgel und Klavier in der Musik des 16. Jahrhunderts* (Leipzig: Breitkopf & Härtel, 1910), p. 14.

[9] Modern fingerings are used in all examples of music.

# SIXTEENTH CENTURY

The following examples of fingering from sixteenth-century sources include a wide variety of patterns. The fingering given in sixteenth-century compositions are relatively few, but there are many fingerings in treatises, usually in the form of scales. The earliest known examples of fingering, including the fingering of a complete composition, are found in Hans Buchner's *Fundamentum*. This important work also includes the fundamentals of keyboard playing, transcriptions of vocal works, and rules of composition.

Buchner's fingerings in *Quem Terra, Pontus, Aethera,* an eleventh-century hymn, often follow the later principle of "good" fingers (2 and 4) on rhythmically strong notes.

## QUEM TERRA, PONTUS, AETHERA[10]

**Whom earth, and sea, and sky**

1. *Fundamentum* (c. 1520)      Hans Buchner (1483–c. 1540)
   Choral in discant

[10] *Geschichte der Musik in Beispielen,* ed. Arnold Schering (Leipzig: Breitkopf & Härtel, 1931), No. 83.

### 2. *Declaración de instrumentos* (1555) [11]  Juan Bermudo (c. 1510–c.1565)

Bermudo stated that the above fingerings could usually be recommended, but that they must be modified when other parts are played with scale passages. However the other parts should be taken with the opposite hand when possible. Ornaments should be played on the beat.

### 3. *Arte de tañer Fantasia* (1565) [12]  Tomás de Sancta Maria (c. 1515–1570)

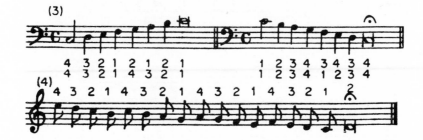

Sancta Maria is the most complete and valuable source for sixteenth-century fingering. He used the thumb freely in both the right and left hands as well as the "conventional" fingerings of his time.

Sancta Maria also gives fingerings for the "short octave" which served to extend the compass of keyboard instruments downward without the additional keys. In the short octave the bass notes C♯ and D♯ were omitted and the F♯ and

11 Kinkeldey, p. 14.
12 Kinkeldey, pp. 28, 36, 38, 39.

G♯ were replaced by D and E. The C was placed on the E key, which became the
bottom note of the octave as follows:

$$D \quad E \quad B♭$$
$$C \quad F \quad G \quad A \quad B \quad C$$

It will be noticed that intervals in the bass as wide as a tenth could be easily
played.

4. *Orgel oder Instrument Tabulatur*      Elias N. Ammerbach (c. 1530–1597)
(1571) [13]

Articulation and phrasing are indicated by the repetition of the same finger
on consecutive notes.

5. *Obras de musica* (1578) [14]        Antonio de Cabezón (1500–1566)

Antonio's organ works were arranged in order of difficulty and published
with examples of fingerings by his son Hernando.

6. *Il Transilvano* (1593) [15]        Girolamo Diruta (1557–1612)

The first organ instruction book, Diruta's *Il Transilvano*, 1593, written
in dialogue between Diruta and his student from Transylvania, is also the first

---

[13] Arnold Dolmetsch, *The Interpretation of the Music of the XVIIth and XVIIIth Centuries*
(London, 1915), p. 366.

[14] *Obras de musica para tecla, arpa y vihuela* (Musical works for keyboard, harp and vihuela). (Madrid, 1578), Kinkeldey, p. 113.

[15] *Il Transilvano* (1593), I:7.

book to distinguish between the techniques of organ and harpsichord playing. Diruta's rules for fingering were even more strict than those from the other sources; he avoided the thumb and fifth finger as much as possible, except in intervals and chords.

In his examples of fingering Diruta used the letters B (*Buono*) to indicate the "good" fingers (2 and 4) and C (*Cattivo*) for the bad fingers (1, 3, 5). He used the thumb in both hands in leaps to unaccented notes (1). The thumb was used in the left hand in *tremoli* (2), *tremoletti* (3), and *groppi* (4).[16]

### 7. *Brande champanje* (1599) [17]        Anonymous

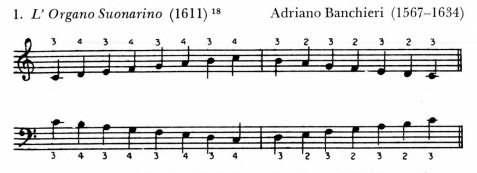

The manuscript of this country dance was owned by Susanne van Soldt, the young daughter of a well-to-do merchant and Protestant refugee from the Netherlands to England. The use of the same finger (3) at the end of the first half bar necessitates a slight separation between the notes. The paired fingerings (3 4) give a natural articulation and stress the dance rhythm. The chords in the left-hand part would be played slightly detached.

## SEVENTEENTH CENTURY

The sixteenth-century principles of fingering in Spain were carried over to seventeenth-century England, the Netherlands, and north Germany with more freedom in the use of the 1st, 3rd and 5th fingers. It is regrettable that there are so few fingerings in the works of the large number of important seventeenth-century keyboard composers.

The following examples of fingerings are in the original sources.

### 1. *L'Organo Suonarino* (1611) [18]        Adriano Banchieri (1567–1634)

This was a practical book primarily designed for the use of church organists.

[16] Catharine Crozier. *The Principles of Keyboard Technique in Il Transilvano by Girolamo Diruta.* Eastman School of Music thesis, 1941, pp. 31, 38, 34, 36.

[17] *Monumenta Musica Neerlandica* III, No. 1, ed. Alan Curtis (Amsterdam: Vereniging voor Nederlandse Muziekgeschiedenis, 1961), p. 3, meas. 1, 2.

[18] *L'Organo Suonarino* (Venice, 1611), V:42.

### 2. *Pavana*[19]  John Bull (1562–1628)

### 3. *Galiarda*[20]  John Bull (1562–1628)

The beginning of each group of ascending sequences is indicated by a "good" finger (2). The second measure shows a glissando with the 4th finger.

### 4. *Ach du feiner Reiter*[21]  Samuel Scheidt (1587–1654)

The above example shows the rapid repetition of notes to produce the effect of a tremolo or vibrato.

[19] *The Fitzwilliam Virginal Book*, 2 vols., J. A. Fuller Maitland and W. Barclay Squire, eds. (New York: Dover Publications, 1963), I:126, meas. 49–52.
[20] *The Fitzwilliam Virginal Book*, I:70, meas. 9–11.
[21] *Tabulatura Nova* (Hamburg, 1624). *Denkmäler deutscher Tonkunst*, (a.) I:62, meas. 1–2; (b.) I:63, meas. 18–19.

## 5. *Echo Fantasia*[22]  Jan Pieterszoon Sweelinck (1562–1621)

The change of keyboards was not indicated in the original, but is shown in the fingering and title. The ornaments may be interpreted as mordents.

[22] *Opera Omnia*, Vol. I, *The Instrumental Works*, ed. Gustav Leonhardt (Amsterdam: *Vereniging voor Nederlandse Musiekgeschiedenis*, 1968), p. 88. Copyright by G. Leonhardt, A. Annegarn & F. Noske. Reprint permission granted by C. F. Peters Corp., sole selling agents for the U.S.A.

6. *Facultad Orgánica* (1626) [23]    Francisco Correa de Arauxo
(c. 1575–after 1633)

This Spanish composer included a number of examples of fingerings in his large and important work. The fingerings disregard many of the sixteenth-century rules and include fingerings for two upper parts. In the third measure there is a rare example of finger substitution from the 2nd to the 3rd finger. The last two measures show the passing of the 4th over the 5th finger a common fingering today.

7. *Livre d'Orgue* (1665) [24]    Guillaume-Gabriel Nivers (1632–1714)

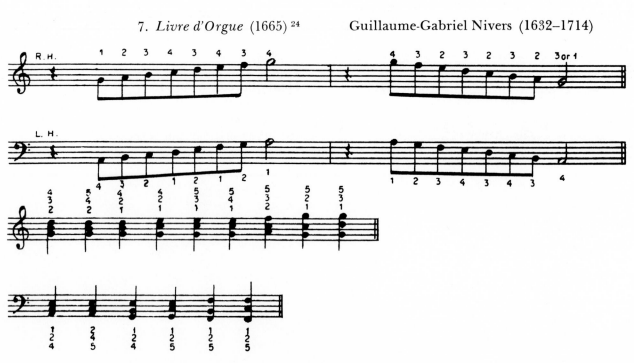

23 *Facultad Orgánica* (Art of Organ Playing)  (Alcalá, 1626) . Charles Jacobs, *Francisco Correau de Arauxo* (The Hague: Martinus Nijhoff, 1973) , pp. 48, 49.
24 *Livre d'Orgue, Contenant Cent Pièces de tous les Tons de l'Eglise* (Paris, 1665)  (*De la position des doigts*) . From a facsimile.

## 8. *Praelude oder Applikatio, Lüneburg Tablatures* (c. 1650) [25]   Anonymous

## 9.  *A Choice Collection of Lessons* (1696) [26]   Henry Purcell (1659–1695)

[25] *The Free Organ Compositions,* from the *Lüneburg Tablatures,* ed. John R. Shannon, II:89.
Copyright 1958 by Concordia Publishing House. Used by permission.
[26] Dolmetsch, p. 392.

10. *Wegweiser* (1692) [27]          Johann Speth? (1664–after 1719)

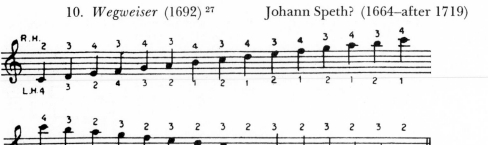

The *Wegweiser,* a work probably known to Bach, and Diruta's *Il Transilvano* (1593) were the only instruction books published before the eighteenth century that were devoted to the organ.

Speth follows the older principle of using the "good" fingers (2 and 4) on rhythmically strong notes, except in the descending scale in the left hand. There he uses 1 and 3 as "good" fingers, a characteristic of the English school and Sweelinck.

## EIGHTEENTH CENTURY

*"As the better fingers become more perfect, they should be used in preference to the weaker ones, without any regard for the old way of fingering, which must be given up in favor of the good playing expected today."*[28]

François Couperin (1668–1733)

Couperin published *L'Art de toucher le Clavecin* (*The Art of Playing the Harpsichord*) in 1716 and a revised edition in 1717. The *Méthode,* as he called it, includes observations on teaching, developing technique, style, performance practice, a complete table of ornaments, and many examples of fingerings from his own works. It may be assumed that even at the age of twenty-two he had already formulated many of these principles of fingering and that they are applicable to his two organ masses of 1690.

The following examples of music and quotations from *The Art of Playing the Harpsichord* indicate Couperin's conservatism and also his freedom from some of the "old" rules of fingering.

1. "Old" style fingering, pp. 41, 82.

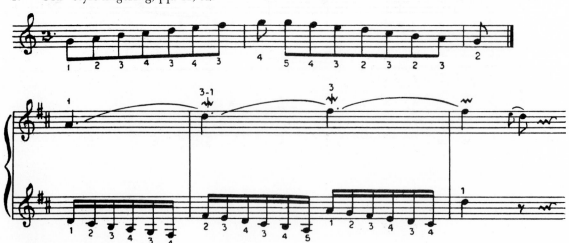

---

[27] *Wegweiser die Orgel recht zu schlagen* (Guide to playing the organ correctly) (Augsburg: Jacob Koppmayer, 1692). pp. 10–11.

[28] *The Art of Playing the Harpsichord,* trans. and ed. by Margery Halford (New York: Alfred Publishing Co., 1974), p. 32.

2. "Modern" style fingering. The fingers pass over the thumb. Phrasing is indicated by wide skips and repeated fingers, p. 83.

3. Consecutive thirds.
"Old" style (non-legato). The fingering placed above the trill sign is for the principal note. All trills begin on the note above the principal note, p. 42.

Modern style (legato). "This way is correct," p. 42.

4. Finger substitution. "Notice how legato this can be played by changing fingers. This requires skill," pp. 51, 53.

5. "Moving by step with the same finger" when the first is half detached ( ▼ ), p. 54.

6.   Moving by step with the same finger to indicate articulation, p. 82. The slurs
     indicate legato, p. 51.

*J. S. Bach (1685–1750)*

"All his [Bach's] fingers were equally skillful; all were equally capable of
the most perfect accuracy in performance. He had devised for himself so con-
venient a system of fingering that it was not hard for him to conquer the greatest
difficulties with the most flowing facility."[29]

There are only two pieces with authentic fingerings by Bach. Both are completely fingered and both are in the *Clavier-Büchlein*[30] that Bach began in 1720
for his eldest son, Wilhelm Friedemann. A *Prelude and Fughetta* (BWV 870a)
has sometimes been attributed to Bach.

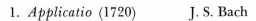

1. *Applicatio* (1720)        J. S. Bach

A facsimile and transcription of the complete *Applicatio* will be found on
pages 28, 29.

In the examples from the *Applicatio,* Bach illustrates the use of finger crossing
with the first and third fingers on the "good" notes, a characteristic of seventeenth-
century English and north German fingerings.

29 *The Bach Reader,* p. 223.
30 J. S. Bach, *Clavier-Büchlein vor Wilhelm Friedemann Bach,* ed. in fascimile by Ralph
Kirkpatrick (New Haven: Yale University Press, 1959) , pp. 9, 20.

## 2. *Praeambulum* (1720)　　　J. S. Bach

The second piece, a *Praeambulum*, is an exercise on broken chords. Bach makes free use of all five fingers, occasional finger crossing, and the thumb on a black key.

A facsimile of the complete *Praeambulum* will be found on page 28.

## 3. *Grundsätze des General-Basses*　　　J. P. Kirnberger (1721–1783)

The above example of two ways that Bach fingered the A-major scale for the left hand was published in 1761 by Johann Philipp Kirnberger (1721–1783) .[31]

31 *The Bach Reader,* p. 450.

47

Kirnberger, Bach's pupil from 1739–1741 in Leipzig, discusses Bach's system of fingering. "Often there are two possible fingerings for a single scale, and one must use now the one and now the other, according to the nature of the piece. The figures above the letters [meant for ascending] can be used in both ascending and descending, as can also the figures below [meant for descending]."

### Carl Philipp Emanuel Bach (1714–1788)

Bach laid the foundation for modern fingering in his *Versuch über die wahre Art das Clavier zu spielen,* 1753. His fingerings form a link between the "old" system, with the emphasis on the use of the 2nd, 3rd, and 4th fingers, and modern fingering with some use of the 5th finger and extensive use of the thumb, "the key to all fingering." His most important innovation, although earlier examples are known, was the "new" method of turning the thumb *under* the 2nd, 3rd, or 4th finger and crossing the fingers *over* the thumb.

The following examples and quotations are from the *Essay.*[32]

1. Old and new fingerings. "None of them is impracticable, although those in which the third finger of the right hand crosses the fourth, the second of the left hand crosses the thumb, and the thumbs strike *f* are perhaps more usual than the others. . . .
[In] the descending scale of C major . . . there are three fingerings, all of which are good in various situations. . . ." (pp. 46, 47).

2. Finger substitution. "Couperin, who is otherwise so sound, calls for replacement too frequently and casually." "We find, at times, that we have too few [fingers]," pp. 72, 73.

3. Slurred notes from a black key to an adjacent white key (glissando), p. 73.

4. Parallel thirds. "Many fingerings are used on thirds, although some are more frequent than others," p. 60.

---

[32] *Essay on the True Art of Playing Keyboard Instruments,* trans. and ed. William J. Mitchell (New York: W. W. Norton, 1951).

5. Broken seconds. "Alternation is better . . . than a repeated finger which causes an excessive detaching of the notes," p. 60.

Bach devoted the first chapter of his *Essay* to the subject of fingering, including examples of scales in all major and minor keys, many with alternative fingerings.

# TOUCH

### Legato—Non-legato—Staccato

*"Every kind of touch has its use."*[33]

Carl Phillip Emanuel Bach

The mastery of all touches through the attack, and especially the release of the keys, is an essential part of an organist's technical and musical equipment. With complete control of finger action and careful listening, all varieties and modifications of legato, non-legato, and staccato can be realized in performance.

The references to touch, as well as other aspects of performance, are always informative, often conflicting, never definitive or exhaustive, and there are many exceptions. A knowledge of these references is important, however, in emphasizing the different viewpoints regarding touch in the early, middle, and late Baroque, and can be helpful in performing music of those periods.

The organ was rarely mentioned, but the word *clavier* in the Baroque generally included the organ with the clavichord and harpsichord. However, the style of the music may indicate one particular instrument.

The general considerations on which the choice of the various touches depends, in addition to the traditional references, are the style (vocal or instrumental), tempo, expressive character, and the use of the music (sacred or secular). The organ (mechanical or electro-pneumatic action) and the acoustics of the room must also be taken into account.

### Legato

Legato is one of the most characteristic touches used in organ playing. The word *legato* as used here means "binding" the notes together without breaks or overlapping. The ideal legato produces a singing line with a continuous flow of sound, vital and plastic.

Slurs, indicating legato in string bowing, were used in keyboard music early in the seventeenth century and are commonly found in the eighteenth century.

1. Girolamo Diruta, *Il Transilvano* (1593). "One does not hold down the notes any more or less than the duration of note values." Diruta illustrates "what happens when a careless organist who, by lifting his hand and striking the keys, loses half of the harmony."[34]

---

[33] *Essay,* p. 149, No. 6.
[34] *Il Transilvano,* I, 5 verso.

The example below, a facsimile from the original edition, is marked "correct," the second "incorrect."[35]

# Tranſiluano Dialogo

2. Costanzo Antegnati, *L'Arte organica* (1608). The Fiffaro "must be played adagio with slow tempo; and the *ripieno* as legato as possible."[36]

3. Samuel Scheidt, *Tabulatura Nova* (1624). "When the notes are connected like this 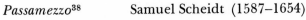 it is a special kind of playing such as the violists do in sliding with the bow. For why should such a manner of playing by the most distinguished violists in the German Nation not be usable, when it gives also to soft-sounding organs, regals, clavicymbaln [harpsichords], and instruments [clavichords] a truly lovely and pleasant effect, on which account I have grown to like this style of playing [legato] and have become accustomed to it."[37]

*Passamezzo*[38]          Samuel Scheidt (1587–1654)

*Toccata, In te Domine speravi*[39]          Samuel Scheidt

35 *Il Transilvano,* I, 5 verso.
36 *L'Arte organica* (Brescia: Francesco Tabaldino, 1608), 8 *verso.*
37 *Tabulatura Nova,* I, 84.
38 *Tabulatura Nova,* I, 45, meas. 1–3.
39 *Tabulatura Nova,* I, 151, meas. 190–192.

In the above example note the non-legato in the first phrase in each measure, imitated by legato sixteenth notes in pairs.

4. Girolamo Frescobaldi, *Fiori musicali* (1635). "The *cantus firmi* should be played legato. For greater convenience, one may also play them detached to make it easier and to avoid too great an inconvenience for the hands. This permission will be used according to the growing skill of the organist."[40]

5. André Raison, *Premier Livre d'Orgue* (1688). "The *Grand Plein Jeu* is played very slowly. The chords should be smoothly connected, never lifting one finger until the other is pressed down. The Voix Humaine is played tenderly and very legato."[41]

6. François Couperin, *L'Art de toucher le Clavecin* (1716), p. 36. The example below illustrates legato notes grouped by slurs. Note the unusual use of a slur over the bar line.

7. J. S. Bach, *Inventiones* (1723). Bach stressed the importance of learning "to play clearly in two voices . . . and above all to arrive at a singing style in playing."[42]

8. Ernst Ludwig Gerber, *Tonkünstler-Lexicon* (1812). Gerber, whose father was one of Bach's pupils, wrote that a certain well-known organist by the name of Schröter "could not possibly please those who knew Bach's *legato* manner of playing, for he [Schröter] played everything staccato."[43]

9. Daniel Gottlob Türk, *Klävierschule* (1789). "In Notes which are to be played *legato,* the finger must remain upon the Key, till the Time of the length of the Note is perfectly expired, so that not the least Separation or Rest may be heard."[44]

### Non-legato

Non-legato as used here refers to a touch with only a slight separation between the notes. This touch, sometimes called a "clear legato," should not be confused with staccato. Clarity in the performance of organ music has always

[40] *Fiori Musicali di Diverse Compositioni* (Venice: Allesandro Vincenti, 1635). "To the Reader."

[41] From a facsimile of the Preface: "Comme il faut donner le mouvement et L'air à toutes les Pieces."

[42] *The Bach Reader,* p. 86.

[43] *The Bach Reader,* p. 186 (n. 77).

[44] Robert Donington, *The Interpretation of Early Music* (London: Faber and Faber, 1977), p. 480.

been a concern of capable organists and teachers. Sancta Maria devoted an entire chapter in his *Arte de tañer Fantasia* (1565) to the way of playing clearly and distinctly. Students should remember the many factors which influence the choice and amount of non-legato necessary to obtain that clarity. A continuous detached style is as monotonous and unmusical as a continuous legato.

The following quotations from eighteenth-century sources show a predilection for the use of non-legato touch.

1. Johann Nicolaus Forkel, *Life of Johann Sebastian Bach* (1802). In explaining why Bach's clavier playing was so much admired, Forkel wrote that "in order to make the delivery perfect [as with Bach] . . . the greatest distinctness [clarity] is required in the production of tones. . . . But this distinctness is susceptible of various degrees."[45] Forkel based his remarks on information from two of Bach's sons, Carl Philipp Emanuel and Wilhelm Friedemann.

2. Friedrich W. Marpurg, *Anleitung* (1755). "Opposed to legato as well as to staccato is the ordinary movement [non-legato] which consists of lifting the finger quickly from the last key shortly before touching the next note. This ordinary movement, which is always understood is never indicated."[46]

3. Carl Philipp Emanuel Bach, *Essay* (1753). "There are many who play stickily, as if they had glue between their fingers. Their touch is lethargic; they hold notes too long. Others in an attempt to correct this, leave the keys too soon. . . . Both are wrong. Midway between these extremes is best.

   "In general the briskness of allegros is expressed by detached notes and the tenderness of adagios by broad, slurred [legato] notes . . . even when a composition is not so marked."[47]

4. Daniel Gottlob Türk, *Klavierschule* (1789). "If notes are to be played in the common way [ordinary movement]; that is to say, neither *staccato* nor *legato,* the fingers must be lifted a little sooner than the Time of the length of the Note is expired."[48]

   Türk was a pupil of Gottfried August Homilius, who was a pupil of J. S. Bach.

### Staccato

Staccato has been used in keyboard music of all periods. In early keyboard music it was indicated by rests, but by the seventeenth-century a dash ( ˈ ) or wedge ( ˈ ) was placed over notes to be played staccato. The dot ( • ) gradually became the principal sign for staccato in the eighteenth-century.

Staccato notes are frequently used in articulation and sometimes in more extended passages and complete compositions.

1. J. S. Bach. Bach used staccato to indicate articulation in several of his organ works (see page 54). The following is one example:
   *Prelude in B minor* (BWV 544, meas. 20–21)

---

45 *The Bach Reader,* p. 307.
46 *Anleitung zum Clavierspielen* (Berlin, 1755) (Method of Keyboard Playing), Donington, p. 479.
47 *Essay,* p. 149.
48 *Klavierschule, oder Anweisung zum Klavierspielen für Lehrer und Lernende* (Leipzig and Halle, 1789) (Keyboard School, or Instruction in Playing for Teacher and Student), Donington, p. 480.

2. Johann Joachim Quantz, *Versuch*, 1752. "Since, however, an entire piece is at present rarely composed in a single species of notes, and we take care to include a good mixture of different types, little strokes are written above those which require the *staccato*. . . . If little strokes stand above several notes, they must sound half as long as their true value."[49]

3. C. P. E. Bach, *Essay*, 1753. "Notes are detached with relation to: (1) their notated length, that is, a half, quarter, or eighth of a bar; (2) the tempo, fast or slow; and (3) the volume, forte, or piano. Such tones are always held for a little less than half their notated length."

   "Tones which are neither detached, connected, nor fully held are sounded for half their value. . . . Quarters and eighths in moderate and slow tempos are generally performed in this semi-detached manner."[50]

4. Daniel Gottlob Türk, *Klavierschule*, 1789. "In Notes which are to be played *staccato*, the fingers must be lifted, when almost half the Time of their length is expired, the other half is filled up by Rests."[51]

5. Johann Christian Kittel, *Grosse Präludien*. Kittel, Bach's last pupil, indicated staccato in No. VII of his collection of Preludes with a dot and also a rest half the value of the note. The second example from the same piece includes staccato and legato articulations.

## PHRASING

The phrase represents a musical thought; phrasing is rendering that thought so that it is meaningful. The end of a phrase is marked by a slight rest taken from the value of the last note of the phrase. Never anticipate the beginning of the next phrase.

An understanding of the relation of each phrase to the structure of each section and the entire composition is necessary in interpreting music of all periods. Phrasing involves harmony, counterpoint, and rhythm. Many phrases, especially in early music and in the Baroque, are made up of short motives. These motives constitute inner phrases and should be identified but rarely detached.

To determine the phrase structures in a composition, the principal cadences should be identified. These include the authentic (V–I), plagal (IV–I), half (ending on IV or V), and deceptive cadences (V–VI). The authentic and plagal cadences give a feeling of finality, the half-cadence requires continuation, and the deceptive cadence introduces the element of surprise.

In contrapuntal music, phrases may overlap, but longer sections might end with a cadence in all voices before beginning the next section. It will be noticed that phrases in contrapuntal lines frequently begin off the beat, which gives the impression that the music is not beginning but continuing. (This effect is common in the art, as well as the music, of the Baroque.)

Melodic phrases have points of increasing tension (*arsic*), decreasing tension (*thetic*), and rest, These are strongly affected by the harmony which accompanies them. A relaxation of tension may occur at the end of a phrase, but do not make a ritard unless it is called for by the music.

The student must keep in mind that an intellectual and artistic comprehension of the music will lead to a proper balance between the motives, phrases, and sections, of the entire composition. Needless to say, a mechanical action organ aids in realizing the subtleties of phrasing and articulation as well as touch.

---

49 *Versuch einer Anweisung die Flöte traversière zu spielen* (Berlin, 1752). *On Playing the Flute*, trans. Edward R. Reilly (London: Faber and Faber, 1966), p. 232, No. 27.

50 *Essay*, pp. 154, 157.
51 Donington, *Interpretation*, p. 480.

# Manual Technique

## POSITION

The correct position should be taken from the very beginning of study in order to develop the physical control which is essential for technical precision, ease of performance, and rapid progress.

It is absolutely necessary that the bench be properly adjusted and the correct position taken every time the student is seated at the console. Place the bench parallel to the manual keys and in such a position that the feet fall naturally under the knees, with the toes just in front of the black keys. Adjust the height of the bench so that the heel and toe of the foot will rest without strain on the surface of the key. The average height of the bench is twenty inches from the top of the pedal $e$ to the top of the organ bench. When a number of players are using the same organ, the bench should be adjustable, or at the correct height for the shortest person and provided with risers of various heights.

When seated on the bench, the organist should be opposite the exact center of the manual keyboards. In a well-designed console, with sixty-one manual keys and thirty-two pedal keys, the center point of the pedal keys ($e$) will be directly under the center point of the manual keys (the space between $f^1$ and $g^1$).

The center position for the organist may be easily determined by placing the left toe on pedal $c$ and the right toe on pedal $g$. Bring the heels and knees together equidistant from the $c$ and $g$. The body will then be centered with the manual and the pedal keyboards. Always maintain the center position and do not slide on the bench. At a console with a shorter manual and pedal compass the center point must be determined by the organist.

Sit squarely and solidly on the bench, but not so far back that the legs cannot be turned to the right or left with ease. When playing on the manuals alone, the right foot may be placed on the open swell pedal or the toe rest and the left heel hooked on the bar under the bench.

Sit erect with the back straight. Lean slightly forward and relax the shoulders and arms. Let the elbows fall close to the body and avoid tension and unnecessary motions.

### Hand Position

A good hand position is necessary in order to achieve perfect muscular control, flexibility, strength, independence, and vitality of finger action.

1. Place the hands on the keys with the fingers curved, and the tip of each finger under the first joint. Keep the back of the hand parallel to the manual keys, and be careful to avoid lowering the hand toward the little finger. The arm and wrist should be about level with the finger tips, and the knuckles slightly raised above the level of the hand. Avoid extremes, and keep the hand and wrist flexible and relaxed so that the fingers can move with complete freedom.
2. Keep the fingers close to the keys at all times.
3. Press the key down firmly and quickly, and release the key with the same precise movement. Do not raise the finger above the top level of the key. Keep the hand, wrist, and forearm perfectly quiet and relaxed. Avoid "breaking" the nail joint. Do not forget to keep the unused fingers in contact with the keys.

After complete muscular control has been acquired, it will be possible for the organist to vary the time of the release of the key between two consecutive notes, through all varieties of repeated notes, legato, non-legato, and staccato playing, phrasing, articulation, and accents.

The mastery of these principles of organ touch will also make it possible for the organist to secure the best musical results from the various types of key action in use today. These include spring action, "tracker touch," and direct tracker action.

# Manual Exercises

### Attack and Release

1. Practice with each hand alone and then both hands together.
2. Attack and release both notes exactly together. Listen!
3. Vary the tempo of each exercise from slow to moderately fast.
4. Register each exercise, using stops which speak promptly.
5. Practice each exercise in several keys with the same fingering.

### Legato and Detached Notes

1. Give the exact time values to the rests and notes. Release the keys with finger action only.
2. Keep the fingers in contact with the keys at all times.
3. Relax and avoid tension.
4. Practice Exercises 1–5 in several keys.
5. Play the legato notes smoothly and clearly.

## Finger Extension

1. Avoid stretching small hands too far.
2. Practice very slowly and relax frequently.
3. Keep the back of the hand as level as possible with all fingers on the keys.
4. Practice exercises 1, 2, and 4 in several keys.
5. Practice a number of these exercises every day.

### Finger Independence

1. A selected number of these exercises should be practiced every day until they can be played quickly and easily.
2. Practice in various rhythms and articulations  (see page 87) .
3. Practice in several keys.

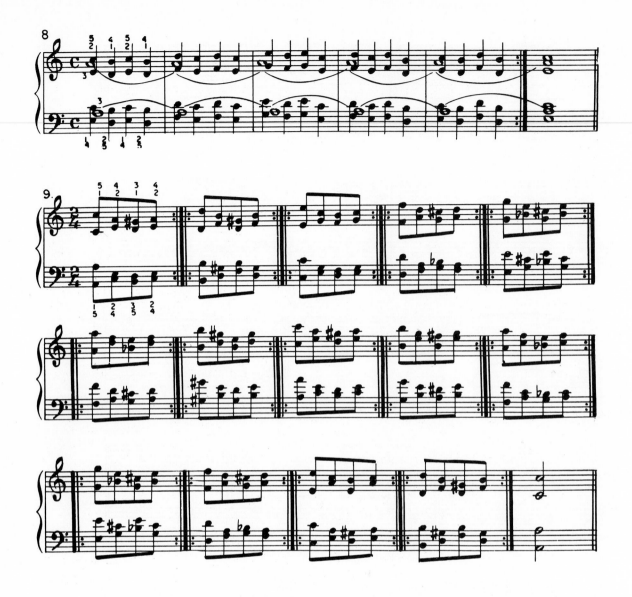

### *Finger Substitution*

All types of finger substitution are useful, particularly in music of the Romantic and modern eras.

1. Substitution on single notes should be made by placing the shorter finger under the longer one.
2. Prepare quickly for the substitution and immediately prepare the proper finger on the next key.

3. Practice slowly at first, counting four eighths to each half note.
4. Gradually increase the tempo, maintaining the same rhythmic substitutions.

### Substitution in Thirds and Sixths

1. Substitution on double notes should be made as illustrated below in Example I or as in Example II.

    a. In Example I, the third and fourth fingers are on one note and the first and second fingers are on the other note at the same time (second eighth of each half note). This method makes it possible to substitute very quickly in rapid tempos and should be given preference.

*b.*   In Example II, the substitution is done successively. This method of substitution may be necessary for small hands, particularly in substitution in sixths.

2.   Transpose Exercises 1 and 3 into all major keys.

3.   Practice slowly at first and gradually increase the tempo.

### Substitution on Common Notes

1. The substitution of fingers should take place separately as illustrated in Example I.
2. Transpose Exercises 1, 2, and 3 into various keys.

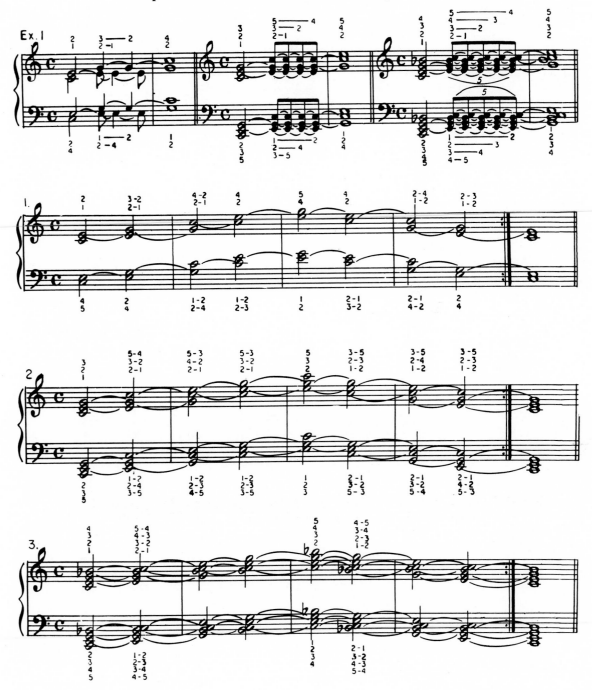

### Substitution in Several Parts

1. Transpose Exercises 1–4 into various keys.

### Glissando

The term *glissando* (with gliding motion), as applied to organ technique, refers to the sliding of the fingers or thumb from one key to another.

The following exercises are divided into two parts:

1. *Finger glissando:* The sliding of the finger (or thumb) off a black key to the adjacent white key above or below it. This may occur with one note or with two, three, or four notes at once.

2. *Thumb glissando:* The sliding and tipping of the thumb in going from one white key to the next white or black key.

### Finger Glissando

1. Slide the finger quickly off the corner or side of the black key without moving the hand or arm.
2. The notes should sound with a clean legato and be in steady time.

### Finger Glissando with Two or More Notes

1. Attack and release every note of each chord at exactly the same instant.
2. Slide off the black key in such a way that all fingers involved will have about the same distance to travel in reaching the white key.
3. Move quickly.

### Thumb Glissando

1. Thumb glissando between two white keys is accomplished as outlined below:
   a. *Descending* with the *right* thumb and *ascending* with the *left* thumb.
      (1) Lower the wrist and place the base of the thumb on the first white key and the tip of the thumb over the next white key.
      (2) With a quick upward motion of the wrist, depress the next white key with the tip of the thumb.

  *b.*  *Ascending* with the *right* thumb and *descending* with the *left* thumb.
    (1)  Raise the wrist and place the tip of the thumb on the first white key and the base of the thumb over the next white key. Keep the thumb straight.
    (2)  With a quick downward motion of the wrist, depress the next white key with the base of the thumb.
 2.  Exercise 1 illustrates both motions of the thumb as explained above.
  *a.*  Hold down the lower key with the base of the thumb and the upper key with the fifth finger. Rock the thumb back and forth by raising and lowering the wrist. Reverse the exercise (b) beginning with the tip of the thumb. Keep the thumb straight.
  *b.*  Maintain a precise rhythm.

### Thumb Glissando from a White Key to a Black Key

 1.  Slide the base of the thumb forward until the tip of the thumb is over the black key.
 2.  Play the black key with the tip of the thumb. Pull the hand back slightly if necessary, and play the following white key with the base of the thumb.

*Thumb Glissando in Thirds, Sixths, and Octaves*

1. Have the base and tip of the finger and the thumb on their respective keys before the attack.
2. Attack and release precisely and hear that all parts sound exactly together.

### Finger Crossing

Finger crossing has always been a useful device in avoiding unnecessary finger substitution.

# Part-Playing

Rhythm, clarity, and vitality have always been essential elements in a musical performance. One of the most important requisites of a performing technique is care in the separation of articulated notes, phrases, and repeated notes.

To separate notes on the piano, it is sufficient to play one note after another at the proper time, since the sound diminishes rapidly in intensity from the moment it is played. However, a note played on the organ continues to sound at the same intensity so long as the key is held down. It is only by releasing the key for a definite interval of time that the separation between notes can be controlled and contribute to a musical performance of organ music.

The student should study every composition and determine the appropriate value of the rests between repeated notes. Often the value of the rests will be equal to the value of the shortest notes which occur most frequently in the composition. Care should be taken to obtain the utmost clarity in playing repeated notes in inner parts, especially in contrapuntal music. The played note and the rest must be equivalent to the full value of the written note.

When the basic principles of playing repeated notes with rests of an exact value have been mastered, the student will have developed control of the release of a note so that all variations of the basic unit will be possible. These variations will normally occur in expressive melodies, for the purpose of accenting a note, at cadences, and between phrases.

It should always be kept in mind that rests as well as notes serve an artistic purpose.

Part-playing includes the techniques of playing repeated notes in various contexts and the interpretation of different types of voice leading in contrapuntal music.

### Repeated Notes of Equal Value

In a series of repeated notes in moderate to fast tempos the rests are half the value of the notes. (Ex. 1:a,b).

Articulations are suggested for the two following examples. The upbeat may also be detached.

(a) *Fugue in C Minor* (BWV 537), Bach

*(b) Fugue in G Major* (BWV 541) , Bach

In slow tempos, or with long notes, the rest will be one-fourth or one-eighth the value of the note. The student should listen carefully and avoid too long a break in the sound, especially in melodic lines. (Ex. 2:a,b) .

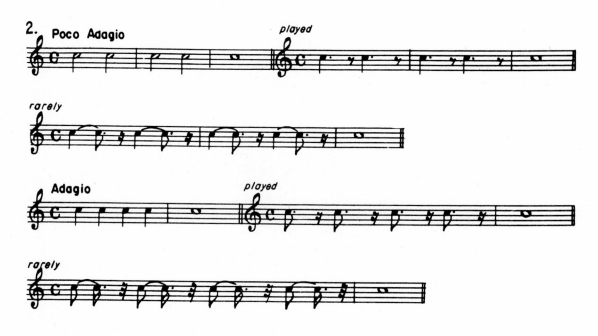

*(a) Herr Christ, der ein'ge Gottes-Sohn* (BWV 601) , Bach

*(b) Diferencias sobre el Canto del Caballero,* Cabezón

### Repeated Notes of Unequal Value

Repeated notes that occur throughout a composition will usually have rests of the same value. Staccato notes are half value (Ex. 3:a).

(*a*) *Magnificat,* Johann Speth

### Repeated Notes in Ternary Rhythm

In ternary rhythm of the following type, the rests are half the value of the note. The suggested articulations are added. The staccato notes should be played half value (Ex. 4:a).

(*a*) *Fugue in G Major* (BWV 577), Bach

### Repeated Dotted Notes

In fast tempos make the rest equal to the value of the dot. In slow tempos, make the rest equal to one half or one quarter the value of the dot (Ex. 5:a,b).

**4.**

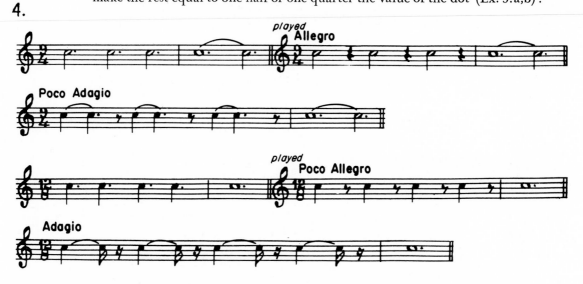

(a) Fughetta super: *Herr Christ, der ein'ge Gottes-Sohn* (BWV 698), Bach

(b) Fughetta super: *Lob sei dem allmächtigen Gott* (BWV 704), Bach

### Tied Notes That Are Repeated

In fast or moderately fast tempos omit the tied note. In slow tempos make the rest half the value of the tied note (Ex. 6:a).

**5.**

(*a*) Fughetta super: *Nun komm' der Heiden Heiland* (BWV 699), Bach

*played*

When a voice enters on a note which has just been sounding in another voice, tie the two voices (Ex. 7:a). If, however, it marks the entrance of a fugal subject or an important theme, make a rest before the entering note (Ex. 7:b).

(*a*) *Fugue in A Major* (BWV 536), Bach

(*b*) *Fugue in G Minor* (BWV 542), Bach

When a voice moves into unison with a stationary note, make a rest in the stationary note (Ex. 8).
Fughetta super: *Herr Christ, der ein'ge Gottes-Sohn* (BWV 698), Bach

*played*

When combined with triplets, the rhythm ♩♪ is usually played ♩³♪ (Ex. 9).
*Prelude in C Minor* (BWV 546), Bach

*played*

The principles of playing repeated notes may be applied when the chord successions are the result of moving polyphonic parts. By lifting the repeated notes and playing the other parts legato, the melodic lines and harmonic progressions will be clarified. (Ex. 10).
*Prelude in G Major* (BMV 541), Bach

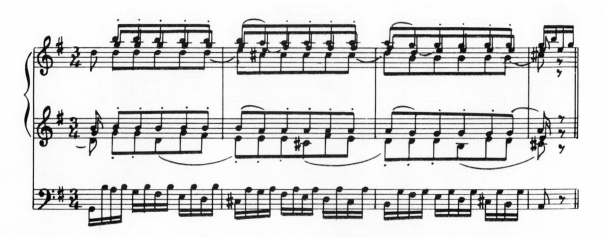

*part four*

# Learning Techniques and Compositions for Manuals

# Learning Techniques

## PRACTICING

It should be the aim of the student to perform each exercise or composition with complete musical understanding and technical perfection. This goal can be achieved only by developing intelligent methods of study and practice until they become habits. The following suggestions will be helpful in acquiring these habits.

1. Make a schedule for daily practice. Devote a definite amount of time to technique, new music, memorizing, and perfecting music already studied. Do not practice too long on one thing and change the order occasionally.

2. Keep a record of the assignment for each lesson and also the compositions learned, memorized, and performed.

3. Devote at least an hour a day to piano practice, especially of technically difficult passages. Use organ finger technique.

4. Concentrate on all the details of the composition, incorporating the articulation, phrasing, and interpretation with the practice. Always use the same fingering and pedaling.

5. Try to avoid playing wrong notes or incorrect time values from the first time an exercise or piece is practiced. If a wrong note or rhythm is played, finish the phrase and then repeat the passage correctly a number of times.

6. Avoid mechanical, unthinking practice and repetition. Always practice after a lesson.

7. Practice slowly in the following sequence: right hand; left hand; both hands; pedal; right hand and pedal; left hand and pedal; both hands and pedal. Begin the slow practice of short sections for both hands and pedal while working on separate parts.

8. When the phrases and sections of a composition have been mastered at a slow tempo, play it all the way through. When this has been accomplished with complete muscular control and accuracy, the tempo may be gradually increased. Return to slow, detailed practice of

sections which are not secure, and repeat this process at succeeding practice periods.

9. Always practice at a steady tempo. Do not play easy passages fast and difficult passages slowly.

10. Devote the most attention to difficult passages.

11. In contrapuntal music, play one or more parts and sing another part.

12. Stop practicing and relax for a few minutes at the first sign of tension.

13. When practicing technical exercises for manuals and pedals, and when first learning a piece, use clear, quick-speaking stops of 8' or 8' and 4' pitch (Gedackt 8', Principal 4').

14. As soon as the notes in a composition have been mastered, work out an appropriate registration.

15. The drawing of stops and the use of mechanical aids when necessary should be carefully practiced in order not to interfere with the performance of the music.

16. The practice of rhythms and articulations in successive groups of notes is invaluable in developing technical control, accuracy, and security, and in increasing tempos. The additional concentration involved is also an aid to memorizing.

Groups of four notes

Groups of three and six notes

Articulations

17. It is of utmost importance that the basic manual and pedal techniques be reviewed and observed in the practice of each composition until these techniques are firmly established.

18. Above all, the student should learn to listen and hear that the parts are sounding together and are released together, and that the phrasing, articulation, touch, rhythm, accents, and interpretation are actually being realized as intended.

## FINGERING

The student should master and make use of all the devices of fingering which will contribute to an effective and musicianly performance of the music. The fingering given in the pieces in *Method of Organ Playing* is designed for hands of average size, but alternate fingerings should be chosen when they are better suited to the student's hand. When the study of music that is not fingered begins, the following suggestions based on the fingering used in *Method of Organ Playing* will be helpful.

1. Do not mark the fingering for every note.
2. When the fingers play consecutive notes directly beneath them, mark the finger only on the first note of the series.
3. Mark the fingering at the points where the thumb turns under the fingers, or the fingers cross over the thumb.
4. Indicate repetitions of the same finger, finger or thumb glissando, finger substitution, and when a finger is extended or contracted from the basic position of the five fingers over five consecutive notes.
5. Avoid substitution of fingers when unnecessary, especially in rapid tempos and on short notes.
6. Make use of finger-crossing of various types when that technique is thoroughly mastered and the musical line is not disrupted.
7. Divide inner parts between the hands when necessary to preserve a legato or facilitate performance.
8. Consider the fingering in relation to the articulation and phrasing, sometimes using the same finger on consecutive notes when moving to a new hand position.
9. The fingering should be related to the final tempo of the composition.
10. Memorize the fingering as quickly as possible and concentrate on the music.

## TOUCH

It should be emphasized again that very early in the student's training the precise playing of various touches and detached notes should be developed. This will make possible the controlled use of the many subtle variations in the value of notes and rests which contribute to all musical performances.

The control of the fingers in legato, non-legato, and staccato playing has already been prepared by the exercises in attack and release (Part III; see also the section on "Touch" in Part II, page 49).

The mastery of all touches requires a sensitive ear and careful listening. The wrist should be kept relaxed and the fingers close to the keys.

1. In legato playing consecutive notes will be connected in such a way that each note will be heard immediately after the one before without overlapping or separation.
2. The notes in non-legato playing will be slightly separated by releasing the first key just before the next key is depressed. The amount of separation between the notes cannot be counted, but it can be heard and will normally be closer to legato than to staccato.

    In order to hear the sound of non-legato notes, play a series of notes on the white keys with one of the fingers, making the interval between the notes as short as possible.

    Practice five-finger exercises non-legato with each hand, in various keys. Begin slowly and gradually increase the tempo.
3. Staccato notes at the beginning of the student's study will be played exactly half value ($\quad$).

There are two methods of playing staccato notes—finger staccato and wrist staccato.

### *Finger Staccato*

1. Finger staccato is most useful in playing one staccato note or a short series of notes.
2. The technique is the same as in the attack and release of a note. The finger should be lifted quickly and precisely.
3. Be careful not to shorten the value of staccato notes, especially in the bass. A non-legato touch is often more appropriate when the bass pipes are slow in speech.

### *Wrist Staccato*

1. Wrist staccato is a most effective way of playing long passages of staccato notes, or chords and entire compositions, without fatigue.

2. Keep the fingers close to the keys and raise and lower the hand from the wrist. The fingers serve only to depress the keys.

3. The fact that the control of the attack and release of the key is at one point, the wrist, rather than the five fingers, makes it possible to play long series of staccato notes exactly half value and without tension.

4. Begin the practice of wrist staccato by placing the hand on the keys and depressing a note with the third finger on the count of "one." On the count of "two" release the key with a slight, quick upward motion of the hand from the wrist, keeping the third finger on the key.

5. Repeat the note with increasing speed, keeping the finger in contact with the key.

6. Continue the practice with all five fingers of both hands until the wrist staccato is firmly established.

### *Marcato*

Marcato touch is usually applied to powerful chords where special accents are desired. The marcato chord is separated from the following chord by a short interval of time, its length depending on the amount of accent desired, usually equivalent to a sixteenth or thirty-second rest.

In releasing marcato or staccato chords there should be a slight pressure on the keys just before the release, bringing the hands up decisively so that all the notes are released at the same instant.

## ACCENTS

Accents in organ playing may be achieved in three ways, all of which are applicable to notes or chords, but will be referred to here as notes.

1. Detach the note before an accent. If the notes before a note to be accented are played non-legato or staccato (half value), slightly lengthen the value of the rest before the accented note. Do not shorten the value of the note.

2. Stress the accented note. Stress (*agogic*) accents are achieved by holding the note to be accented a little longer than the note before and after the accented note. The stress accent marks a slight deviation from the strict tempo and finds its principal application in the molding of a melodic line and inner phrases.

3. Delay the accented note. In a passage leading to an accented note, the previous notes may be increasingly emphasized so that a slight delay before the accented note becomes a part of the whole phrase or section.

The student must be continually on guard not to break the music into episodes or to destroy the fundamental rhythmic pulse and drive of the music.

## MEMORIZING

The principal reason for playing from memory lies in the fact that it will result in a better performance, both technically and musically. The perfectly memorized work becomes a part of the performer and gives him complete freedom of expression.

When a piece of music is practiced correctly and efficiently, it is also being memorized, and good practice habits will lead to a continual improvement in the ability to memorize.

After a composition has been thoroughly learned *with the notes,* the complete process of memory should be undertaken. Concentration and interest in learning are indispensable to the memory process.

There are four types of memory which are used in music. Three of these types—aural, visual, and motor memory—depend on our senses or imagery. The fourth and most important type is known as cognitive memory. It is based on knowledge, and is the memory we use in the analytical study of the music.

The memorization of music requires the combination and collaboration of the four types of memory. We all vary in our natural gifts and capacities, but all types of memory should be cultivated and can be improved.

### *Cognitive Memory*

This memory is the basis of all study, from the time the piece is first practiced until it is performed from memory. Every detail of the music should be analyzed technically and musically, and be consciously known.

Organize notes into patterns, groups, and phrases. Note all sequences and variations from the sequential pattern. Analyze harmonic progressions and relate them to each other. Contrapuntal lines, rhythm, and interpretative factors are all a part of analytical study. Study the form and relate the details to the whole.

### *Aural Memory*

This memory is useful in enabling us to hear mentally what the next note or chord is, and it strengthens the other types of memory. The ability to hear accurately and retain what we hear should be developed until individual lines of the music can be played and sung without errors. Eventually a whole composition can be "practiced" by going through it and hearing the sound mentally.

### Visual Memory

This type of memory gives us a mental image of the way the notes look on the printed page, or the place of the notes and the shape of each passage on the keyboard. Visual memory may be developed by concentrating on a measure of music, consciously noting all its details, and then reproducing it from the mental image. Gradually more measures can be added, and a mental image of whole phrases and sections can be retained. Avoid using different editions of a composition during the learning process.

### Motor Memory

This is one of the most useful and also the most dangerous types of musical memory. Motor memory involves the touch sensations and training of the muscles so that the movements in playing become automatic. They should, however, never be mechanical.

In developing motor memory the same fingering and pedaling must always be used. Avoid repeating phrases endlessly without thought or purpose.

Never depend on motor memory alone in memorizing a piece. The slightest interruption in the automatic process will inevitably lead to a breakdown.

### Summary

1. Begin to learn the techniques of memorizing with the first lesson. A few of the manual studies in which the student is particularly interested should be memorized after they have been learned perfectly with the music.

2. Memorizing should continue throughout the organist's career and be made a part of every practice period.

3. Memorize when the mind is alert and the power of concentration is strongest. Do not attempt to memorize when fatigued.

4. The more thoroughly the music is learned the longer it will be retained and the more positive will be its recall.

5. In reviewing a work previously memorized always consult the score and repeat the original memory process.

6. Memorize phrases or short sections at first and gradually develop the ability to learn longer sections. Always be sure the sections are connected in the mind and make a unified whole.

7. Work on at least one new section of music each day and then review the previous sections.

8. Memorize landmarks at cadential points and practice beginning at any one of these landmarks.

9. Memorize and be able to play the parts for each hand alone and the pedal part alone.

10. Do not think of difficulties ahead, or the association of chord to chord and phrase to phrase will be lost.

11. In performing from memory, the subconscious mind will function if fear does not intervene.

12. The fear of forgetting can be eliminated by the knowledge that every detail of the music and its interpretation has been engraved in the mind and that the aural, visual, and motor senses have been well trained.

# Compositions for Manuals

The compositions for manuals, and for manuals and pedal, are an application of the manual and pedal techniques, and the beginning of the study of performance practice and interpretation (Part II, p. 19). The compositions in *Method of Organ Playing* have been selected for their musical, as well as technical, value and represent a brief outline of composers and music, particularly from the fifteenth century through the Baroque. The regular study, even if brief, of all subjects related to each composition and composer will lay the foundation for the student's continued growth in knowledge and musicianship.

The student should continue the daily practice of useful technical exercises, and review the sections in Parts I, II, and III which apply to the composition being studied. The technical problems of performance should be solved progressively and always in advance of the composition being performed.

Articulation has been suggested in a few compositions, either by marks or by the fingering and pedaling used. Articulations should be added by the student to other compositions when appropriate. A few compositions have been edited with early fingering; some have only partial fingering which should be completed by the student where necessary.

The art of registration will begin with the first composition studied. The principles of registration (Part I) should be studied and appropriate registration for the music, organ, and period of composition should be worked out by the student.

Students who are also church musicians will find that many of the compositions will be useful as interludes, or combined into suites for preludes in the church service.

# ARIA

**"So oft ich meine Tobackspfeife"**

*Noten-Büchlein vor Anna Magdalena Bach*       Anonymous
        (1725)

# DUO

Allen I. McHose

# DA JESUS AN DEM KREUZE STUND

**As Jesus hung upon the Cross**

*Tabulatura Nova* (1624)    *Versus III*    Samuel Scheidt (1587–1654)

# DUO

*Obras de Música* (pub. 1578)     Antonio de Cabezón (c. 1510–1566)

## AVE MARIS STELLA

*Annuale* (1645)    Giovanni Battista Fasolo
(dates unknown)

# PENTATONIC STUDY

Herbert Elwell

# INTONAZIONE DEL 9° TONO

*Intonazioni d'organo* (1593)　　Giovanni Gabrieli (1557–1612)

## MAGNIFICAT OCTAVI TONI

*Ars magna Consoni et Dissoni* (1693)    Johann Speth (1644–c. 1720)

# CLAUSULA DE TONO V

*Arte de tañer Fantasia* (1565)　　　Fray Tomás de Sancta Maria
(c. 1510/20–1570)

# CLAUSULA DE TONO V WITH GLOSAS

## O CLE [MENS]

*Fundamentum Organisandi* (1452)     Conrad Paumann (c. 1415–1473)

# TU DEVICTO MORTIS

*Tabulature pour le jeu d'orgues* (1531)          Published by Pierre Attaingnant (d. 1552)

# O GOTT, DU FROMMER GOTT

## O God, Thou Faithful God

*Chorale Variation IV*     J. S. Bach (1685–1750)

# A POYNCTE

## A Point

*Mulliner Book* (c. 1545–c.1585)     *Thomas Tallis* (c. 1505–1585)

# RÉCIT DE CORNET

*Messe pour les Couvents* (1690)　　　François Couperin (1668–1733)

# PETITTE FUGUE SUR LE CHROMHORNE

*Messe pour les Couvents* (1690)    François Couperin (1668–1733)

The two pieces of Couperin have been fingered according to Couperin's directions. The *notes inégales* pattern in the *Récit de Cornet* is intended to be used on all eighth-note groups, and the indication of [*detaché*] (*notes égales*) should be followed throughout the *Petitte Fugue*.

# Fughetta super:
## *GOTTES SOHN IST KOMMEN*

**God's Son has come**

J. S. Bach (1685–1750)

## Fughetta super:
# HERR CHRIST, DER EIN'GE GOTTES-SOHN

**Lord Jesus Christ, the Only Son of God**

J. S. Bach (1685–1750)

# LOBT GOTT, IHR CHRISTEN ALLZUGLEICH

**Praise God, ye sons of men**

*Chorale Variation I*

Johann G. Walther
(1684–1748)

# Fughetta super:
## LOB SEI DEM ALLMÄCHTIGEN GOTT

**Praised be Almighty God**

J. S. Bach (1685–1750)

## BENEDICIMUS TE

*Second Livre d'Orgue* (1678)     Nicolas Le Bègue (1630–1702)

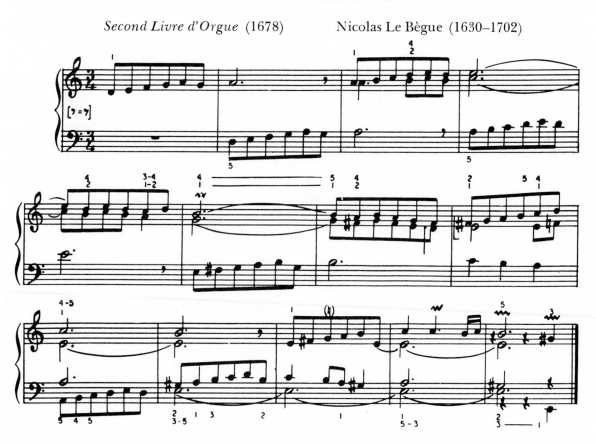

The eighth-note groups may be divided into pairs of slurred notes and played
with a pattern similar to (see *Notes inégales,* p. 34).

# WER NUR DEN LIEBEN GOTT LÄSST WALTEN

**If thou but suffer God to guide thee**

J. S. Bach (1685–1750)

## GLORIFICAMUS TE

*Second Livre d'Orgue* (1678)          Nicolas Le Bègue (1630–1702)

115

# VATER UNSER IM HIMMELREICH

**Our Father Who art in Heaven**

*Clavierübung III* (1739)  J. S. Bach (1685–1750)

# TRIO EN PASSACAILLE

*Messe du II<sup>e</sup> Ton* (1688)          André Raison (c. 1640–1719)

* The *coulé* is illustrated in the table by Le Bègue (page 21).

part five

# Pedal Technique
# and Pedal Exercises

## Studies for Manuals and Pedal

Selected from Part VI (pages 165–168).

### Alternate Toes

*Each Foot Moves the Interval of a Third*

1. When both feet are playing at the extremes of the pedalboard, it may be necessary to turn the body by pressing against the key with the left toe ascending and the right toe descending.

2. Transpose Exercises 1 and 2 into the following major keys: D, E-flat, E. Change the key signature as indicated in the following examples:

3. Keep the knees and heels together and move both feet at the same time.

**Heel and Toe**

1. In Exercise 4, the rests between the repeated eighth notes should be sixteenths.
2. Keep the ankles turned in at all times.

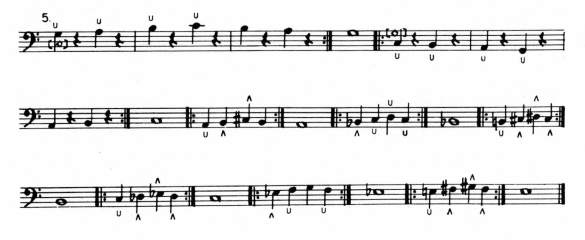

### Compositions for Manuals and Pedal

Selected from Part VI (pages 169–174).

### Alternate Toes

*Each Foot Moves the Interval of a Fourth*

1. Practice four-note groups in all rhythms and articulations (page 87).
2. Practice six-note groups as follows:

3. Transpose Exercise I into the following major keys: G, B-flat, D. Change the key signature as indicated in the following examples:

131

4. Move both feet at the same time.

**Heel and Toe**

**Compositions for Manuals and Pedal**

Selected from Part VI.

*Alternate Toes*

*Each Foot Moves the Interval of a Fifth*

1.  Practice four-note groups in all rhythms and with the following articulations:

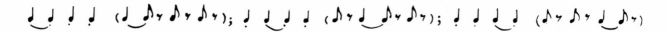

2.  Keep the knees touching and separate the heels slightly for the interval of a sixth.

3.  Transpose Exercise 1 into the following major keys: D-flat, D, E-flat, F, G, A-flat, B-flat. Change the key signature as indicated in the previous examples.

4. Transpose Exercise 7 above into the following major keys: D-flat, D, E-flat, F, G, A-flat, B-flat. Change the key signature as indicated in the following examples:

1. The pedaling in the following exercise is based on the complete scale.
2. Keep the feet together and *do not cross* one foot *over* the other.

### Compositions for Manuals and Pedal

Selected from Part VI.

### Alternate Toes

*Each Foot Moves the Interval of a Sixth*

1. Practice four-note groups in all rhythms and articulations (page 87).

2. Transpose Exercises 1 and 2 into the following major keys: D-flat, D, E-flat, F, G, A-flat. Change the key signature as indicated in the previous examples.

3. Transpose Exercise 4 into the following major keys: D-flat, D, E-flat, F, G, A-flat, B-flat. Change the key signature as indicated in the previous examples.

### *Toes Only—Heel and Toe*

1. Practice Exercises 1 and 2 with toes only. Playing consecutive notes as well as intervals with toes only is a part of modern, as well as Baroque, pedal technique and is especially useful in playing non-legato.
2. Move the foot to the next note as quickly as possible.

3. The pedaling in the following exercise is based on the complete scale. Keep the feet close together and do not cross one foot over the other.

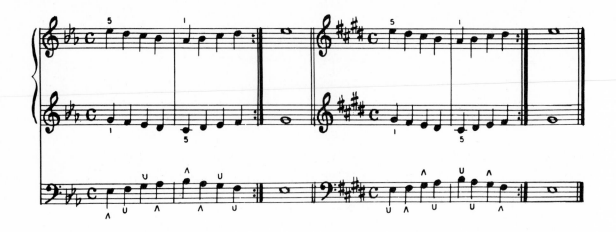

Selected from Part VI.

### Exercises Based on Pedal Parts in Compositions by J. S. Bach

The student should add articulations where appropriate.

1. *Alle Menschen müssen sterben*

2. *Es ist das Heil uns kommen her*

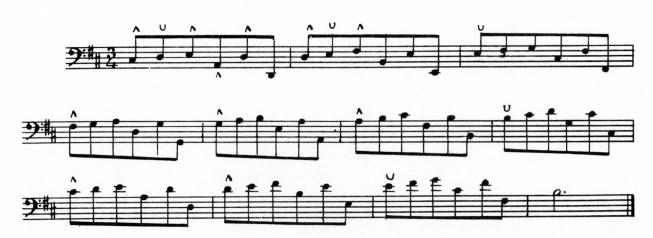

### 3. *In dir ist Freude*

### 4. *Fugue in G Minor*

### 5. *Herr Christ, der ein'ge Gottes Sohn*

6. *Sonata in E-flat Major*

7. *Fugue in D minor*

8. *Prelude in A minor*

### Pedal Glissando

*From a Black Key to a White Key*

1. Slide the toe quickly off the black key.
2. Keep the heel low and avoid making unnecessary noise.
3. Keep the ankle turned in.
4. Maintain perfect time and a clean legato.

*Alternate Toes in Wide Intervals*

151

### Broken Chords

1. Prepare each note by placing the heel or toe as quickly as possible over the next note to be played by that foot.
2. Practice with each foot alone.

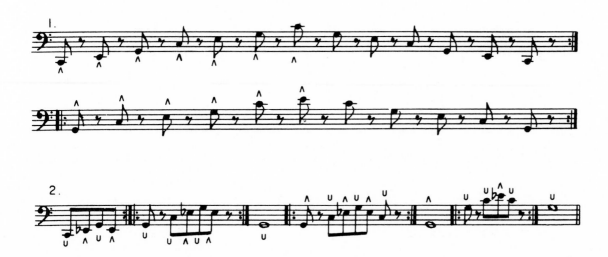

3.   Practice two notes together with each foot.

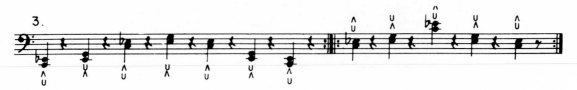

4.   Practice with both feet together.

## PEDAL EXERCITUM

J. S. Bach (1685–1750)

**Double Notes**

*Thirds*

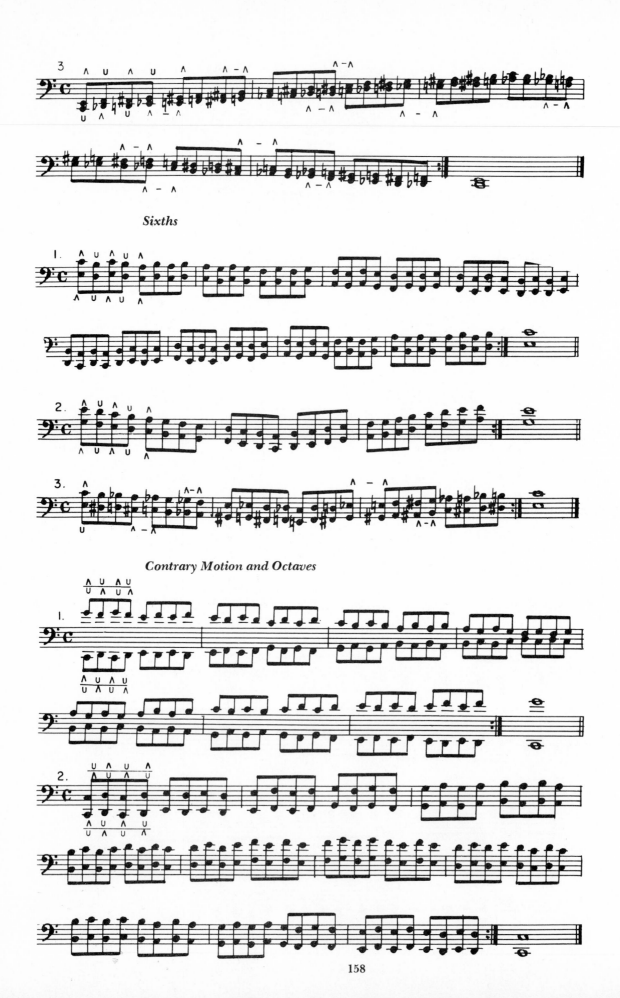

*Sixths*

*Contrary Motion and Octaves*

158

*Chords*

159

*part six*

# Studies and Compositions for Manuals and Pedal

Two Perpetual Canons
on

## *FREU' DICH SEHR, O MEINE SEELE*

**(Rejoice greatly O my soul)**

Thomas Canning

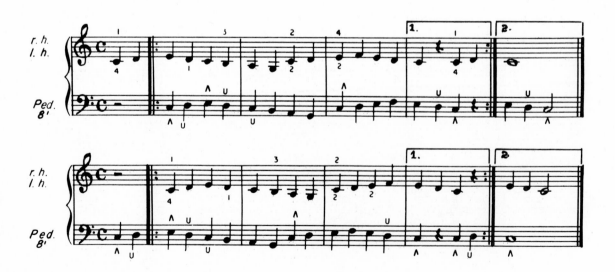

Transpose to D Major

## *AUS TIEFER NOTH SCHREI' ICH ZU DIR*

### (From deepest need I cry to Thee)

Wayne Barlow

## *AUS TIEFER NOTH SCHREI' ICH ZU DIR*

### (From deepest need I cry to Thee)

Wayne Barlow

## *STUDY FOR LEFT HAND AND PEDAL*

Herbert Inch

This study should be articulated in several different ways and transposed up from one to five semitones.

# CANON

*Dorian Mode*      Allen I. McHose

# VERSET

*Wegweiser* (1692)     Johannes Speth (1664?–c. 1720)

The *Wegweiser die Art die Orgel recht zu schlagen* (Guide to the art of playing the organ correctly) was a popular organ instruction book in central and southern Germany. Bach undoubtedly used this book for his early instruction in organ playing.

# VERSET

*Wegweiser* (1692)     Johannes Speth (1664?–c. 1720)

# ERMUNTRE DICH, MEIN SCHWACHER GEIST

**(Arouse thyself, my weak spirit)**

Wayne Barlow

# ERSCHIENEN IST DER HERRLICHE TAG

**(The glorious day has dawned)**

Wayne Barlow

# WENN WIR IN HÖCHSTEN NÖTHEN SEIN

**(When we are in utmost need)**

Johann Christoph Bach (1642–1703)

# VOM HIMMEL HOCH, DA KOMM' ICH HER

**(From Heaven above to earth I come)**

Friedrich Wilhelm Zachau (1663–1712)

From 80 Chorale Preludes,
ed. Hermann Keller (New York:
C. F. Peters Co., 1937), p. 109.

## JESU, NUN SEI GEPREISET

**(Jesus, now be praised)**

Wayne Barlow

# AGNUS DEI

*Messe pour les couvents* (1690)  François Couperin (1668–1733)

Man.

Ped.

# VATER UNSER IM HIMMELREICH

### (Our Father Who art in Heaven)

Johann Krieger (1651–1735)

# AUS TIEFER NOTH SCHREI' ICH ZUR DIR

## (From deepest need I cry to Thee)

*Ariadne Musica* (1702)          J. K. F. Fischer (c. 1670–1746)

## FUGA

*Blumen-Büschlein* (1699)          J. K. F. Fischer (c. 1670–1746)

## CANON

*École d'orgue* (1862)        Jacques Lemmens (1823–1881)

# PRAEAMBULUM

Gottlieb Muffat (1690–1770)

# TOCCATA AVANTI LA MESSA DELLA MADONNA

*Fiori Musicali* (1635)          Girolamo Frescobaldi (1583–1643)

The *Fiori Musicali* was originally published in a four-part score.

# VERSET

*Wegweiser* (1692)        Johannes Speth (1664?–c.1720)

Adapted from the *Annuale* by Giovanni Battista Fasolo (1645).

# PREAMBULUM IN RE

*Orgeltabulaturbuch* (c. 1524)        Leonhard Kleber (c. 1490–1556)

Man. to Ped. only

# JESU, MEINE FREUDE

### (Jesus, my Joy)

Wayne Barlow

# MEINE SEELE ERHEBT DEN HERREN

**(My soul doth magnify the Lord)**

*Magnificat Mariae*          Johann Pachelbel (1653–1706)

# PENTATONIC STUDY

Herbert Elwell

# TOCCATA AVANTI LA MESSA DELLA DOMENICA

*Fiori Musicali* (1635)  Girolamo Frescobaldi (1583–1643)

The *Fiori Musicali* was originally published in a four-part score.

# JESU, MEINE FREUDE

### (Jesus, my Joy)

*Partita VI*          Johann G. Walther (1684–1748)

# VOM HIMMEL HOCH, DA KOMM' ICH HER

**(From Heaven above to earth I come)**

Gustav Merkel (1827–1885)

# DEPOSUIT POTENTES

*Verset from the Magnificat* (1626)       Jean Titelouze (1563–1633)

# ALLEIN GOTT IN DER HÖH' SEI EHR'

### (All Glory be to God on High)

Andreas Armsdorff (1670–1699)

*From* Orgelchoräle um Joh.
Seb. Bach, *ed. Gotthold
Frotscher (Leipzig: Edition
Peters, 1937), p. 13.*

# MISSA APOSTOLORUM

*Intabulatura* (1543)
*Et in terra pax*

Girolamo Cavazzoni (c. 1520–c. 1577)

The *Missa Apostolorum* was originally written for manuals alone.

## Benedicimus te

## Quoniam tu solus

# WARUM BETRÜBST DU DICH, MEIN HERZ

### (Why dost thou grieve, my heart?)

*Versus III*        Samuel Scheidt (1587–1654)

## *FUGATO*

J. G. Albrechtsberger (1736–1809)

# TRIO

Johann Ludwig Krebs (1713–1780)

196

# PREMIER SANCTUS EN TAILLE À 5

*Livre d'Orgue* (1699)    Nicolas de Grigny (1672–1703)

# O PIA

### (O Clemens)

*Tabulaturen etlicher Lobgesang* (1512)  Arnolt Schlick (c. 1450–c. 1525)

The scale pedaling follows Schlick's suggestions in his *Spiegel der Orgelmacher und Organisten* (1511). The double pedal should be played with a very
short break between the notes.

# LOBET DEN HERREN

**(Praise ye the Lord)**

Wayne Barlow

# NUN KOMM' DER HEIDEN HEILAND

### (Come now, Redeemer of our Race)

Dietrich Buxtehude (1637–1707)

203

# LOBT GOTT, IHR CHRISTEN, ALLZUGLEICH

**(Praise God, all ye Christians)**

*Partita III*     Johann G. Walther (1684–1748)

*From* The Church Organists'
Golden Treasury *II, Carl F.
Pfatteicher and Archibald
Davison, eds. (Bryn Mawr,
Pa.: Theodore Presser Co.,
1950) II: 151.*

## SCHMÜCKE DICH, O LIEBE SEELE

**(Adorn thyself, O my soul)**

Wayne Barlow

# MARIA ZART VON EDLER ART

**(Gentle Mary of noble mien)**

*Tabulaturen etlicher Lobgesang* (1512)          Arnolt Schlick  (c. 1450–c. 1525)

## VON GOTT WILL ICH NICHT LASSEN

**(From God I will not depart)**

Wayne Barlow

# VOM HIMMEL HOCH, DA KOMM' ICH HER

**(From Heaven above to earth I come)**

Georg Böhm (1661–1733)

211

# HERZLICH THUT MICH VERLANGEN

### (My heart is filled with longing)

J. S. Bach (1685–1750)

## SCHMÜCKE DICH, O LIEBE SEELE

(Adorn thyself, O my soul)

Wayne Barlow

# PASTORAL

Leo Sowerby (1895–1968)

# LIEBSTER JESU, WIR SIND HIER

**(Blessed Jesus, we are here)**

J. S. Bach (1685–1750)

*part seven*

# Service Playing

# Service Playing

Playing for a church service has always been one of the organist's most important functions. It can be as rewarding as any part of the organist's profession and demands the utmost musical and technical competence. However, a facile technique and mastery of the organ literature do not prepare one completely for the art of service playing which requires special techniques in the preparation of hymns, accompaniments, and liturgical music. Since many organists are also choirmasters, a knowledge of the techniques of singing and the ability to conduct the choir from the console are indispensable. Modulation, improvisation, and transposition are also important parts of the church musician's equipment and should be cultivated from the beginning of the student's study.

The organ music, hymns, accompaniments for vocal solos, anthems, oratorios, and liturgical music should be prepared with utmost care. All the service music should be of a high quality and related to the season of the church year or the mood of the service.

## HYMN PLAYING

The study of hymn playing should not begin until the student has thoroughly mastered the basic techniques of organ playing. Hymns vary widely in style from plainsong and chorales to gospel songs, and there will always be some exceptions to the general principles of hymn playing.

A strong feeling for rhythm, clarity, the right tempo, and the mood of the words is of first importance in inspiring the congregation to sing.

1. Study the words of the hymn; sing them during practice and when playing in the church service. The words, music, and the season of the church year will determine the mood, phrasing, tempo, touch, registration, and rhythmic pulse.
2. Mark the pedaling and learn the pedal part before practicing the manual parts. Play the pedal part in the octave in which it is written.
3. The tenor part will be played with the left hand, and the bass with the pedal. Also practice the hymn without the pedal, playing the tenor and bass with the left hand.
4. Legato should be the principal touch in hymn playing. A non-legato touch will often be needed in reverberant churches, and detached chords at certain points will be effective when the words suggest strong accents.
5. Study the form, harmonic rhythm, type of melody, note values, and phrase lengths of the music. Play the hymns with understanding and vitality.

### Introduction

1. Processional hymns should preferably be played all the way through before singing. The choir should not march in military formation, but walk naturally and rhythmically.
2. The first and last phrases in familiar hymns may be played for the introduction when harmonically suitable, or the first phrase only, even if it ends on the dominant chord.
3. The tempo of the introduction must be exactly the same as that of the hymn.
4. The time interval between the introduction and the singing of the hymn must be the same as that between stanzas.

### Phrasing

1. The phrase lengths are determined by the meter of the hymn. Long meter (8.8.8.8) has eight syllables in each line of the hymn.
2. All parts are usually phrased with a rest at the end of a line of text.
3. Phrase within a line only when the words require it, but do not make a break at every comma. When the musical phrase does not agree with the punctuation of the text it is preferable to phrase according to the text.
4. At the end of each stanza hold the last chord a full measure, or half a measure, and make

a rest in the same rhythmic pulse before beginning the next stanza. The rhythmic pulse is based on the word accents of the hymn.

5. In chorales and some hymns there may be hold signs marked at cadential points. As a general principle the rhythmic pulse of the held note and the following rest must be preserved. The punctuation of the words and the tempo will determine the proper length of the note marked with a hold and the rest.

6. It is of the utmost importance that the length of rest between stanzas is always the same. Do not ritard at the end of any stanza, except the last, when a slight ritard may be made.

### Tempo

1. Each hymn will have its own particular tempo which will grow out of the study of the words and music.

2. Long phrases require a somewhat faster tempo than short phrases.

3. Do not play hymns metronomically, but with a strong rhythmic pulse.

4. Hymns with many short notes should not be played too quickly, or those with long notes too slowly.

5. Consider the acoustical environment in the church.

### Repeated Notes

1. In order to maintain clarity and a strong rhythmic pulse there should be little, if any, tying of repeated notes.

2. Never tie the soprano part.

3. A series of repeated notes may sometimes be tied in the alto and bass parts from strong to weak beats of the measure.

### Amens

1. An Amen is sung when the phrase "So be it" is appropriate.

2. Hold the final chord of the hymn the same length and rhythmic pulse as between stanzas. Tie the common note between the final chord and the Amen and release the other notes of the chord on the rest.

3. The Amen is usually played legato, or the three lower voices may be lifted, separating the two syllables of the Amen.

4. Play the Amen in a positive manner and in the tempo of the hymn.

5. Do not reduce the volume of the organ for the Amen.

### Registration

1. While it is possible to overdo changes of registration, the reverse can be dull and uninspiring. Avoid playing every hymn with the same registration and in the same manner.

2. The general character of the words, the size of the congregation and church, and the acoustics should be taken into consideration in selecting a suitable registration. Make sure that the registration is strong enough to lead the singing.

3. The registration should be a bright, clear forte based on the Great principal chorus. It may be necessary to couple other manuals to the Great in order to strengthen or brighten the tone.

4. Reeds may be added for the more brilliant hymns, or for one or two climactic stanzas when the words and music are appropriate. The occasional omission of the pedal part, playing all four parts on the manuals, will provide relief and variety, especially in the longer and more quiet hymns.

5. The hymn tune may be played as a solo with a powerful reed or combination. The alto and tenor parts will be played by the left hand on another manual.

6. One stanza may sometimes be sung without the organ. The choir should be well rehearsed and the congregation informed by a note in the service leaflet.

### Free Accompaniments, Descants, and Interludes

1. The occasional use of free accompaniments and descants will provide variety and stimulate congregational singing.

2. Free accompaniments and descants are most effective in well-known hymns, but should not be used on more than one or two stanzas of a hymn. The climactic stanzas, frequently the last or next-to-last stanza, are usually most suitable for free accompaniments and descants.

3. Descants may be sung by all or part of the soprano section, or played by the organist as part of a free accompaniment.

4. Faux-bourdon settings may be either sung or played.

5. During long processionals, interludes between the stanzas of the hymn are often used. The interludes should be played strictly in time, in

the style of the hymn, and consist of at least eight measures. When an interlude is to be used, do not make a break at the end of the stanza but begin the interlude on the last beat of the stanza without a pause. Lead back unmistakably to the beginning of the next stanza. The ideal way to conclude the interlude is to repeat part or all of the last phrase of the hymn. It is also effective to end the interlude on the dominant chord, preceded by a *slight* ritard.

6. Do not play interludes between stanzas that express one thought.
7. Using an interlude to raise the pitch for the last stanza is unmusical and theatrical.

The following Advent hymn, adapted from a melody by Christian Friedrich Witt (1715) with text by Charles Wesley (1744), will serve as an example of some of the basic principles of hymn playing.

## STUTTGART

87. 87

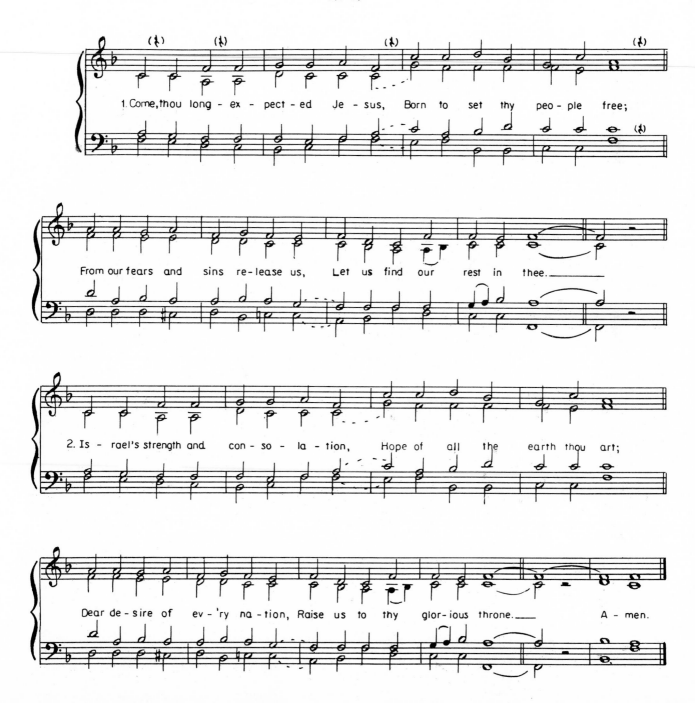

## ADAPTING PIANO ACCOMPANIMENTS

### *Basic Principles*

1. The arrangements of piano scores must be idiomatically effective on the organ.
2. Widely separated notes, octaves, and chords should be brought into the middle range of the keyboard. Avoid thick chords in low registers.
3. Observe the musical values of the piano score. These include rhythm, phrasing, characteristic figurations, accents, and written instructions.
4. Preserve the motion of the music, and do not reduce all pianistic devices to chords.
5. Rapid bass passages may be played on the manuals with the 16′ pedal playing only the accented beats.
6. Passages with a clearly defined bass line may be played with 16′ pedal, and even 32′ when appropriate.
7. When playing a bass line written in octaves it is usually better to play the upper note. This will preserve the integrity of the bass line, and will prevent the monotony of all notes sounding in the lower octave.
8. Avoid heavy, dull 8′ and 4′ stops on the manuals and the continual use of 16′ stops in the pedal. Flute tone is most effective in higher pitches and will usually make the doubling of chords unnecessary.
9. The registration should be bright, clear, well balanced, and appropriate to the style of the music.
10. Solo and chorus reeds, mutations, and even célestes have their use when they are suitable to the character and style of the music.

### *Arpeggios*

1. Pianistic, arpeggiated chords may be played by holding the chords of the harmony with the left or right hand and playing the arpeggiated chords with the other hand within a narrow range.

2. Stops of 8′, 4′, and 2′, or 8′ and 2′ pitches will often be effective in the right hand when playing arpeggiated chords. Use 8′ and 4′ in the left hand coupled to the pedal 16′.

### *Repeated Chords*

1. Repeated chords follow the general principles of accompanying from piano scores as outlined above.

2. Repeated chords in both hands may be played by holding some notes of the chord and repeating others.

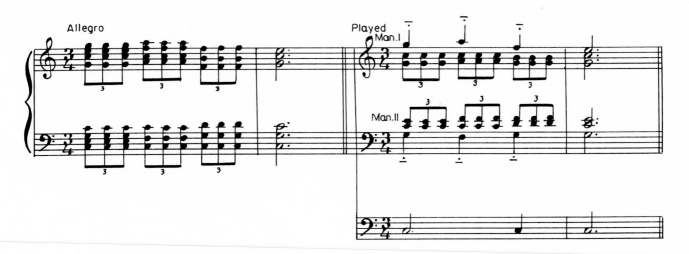

### Tremolos

Tremolos in either or both hands may be played by sustaining one or two outer voices of the chord and playing the other notes as indicated in the score. The pedal repeats the bass notes of the chords. In certain cases, a better effect may be achieved by the rapid alternation of notes an octave apart. Occasionally it may be effective, in simulating the roll of the tympani, to hold the bass note simultaneously with the note a half step below.

### Oratorio Scores

1. Oratorio scores arranged for piano can be only an approximation of the orchestral score and often will need to be considerably simplified.
2. A study of the orchestral score, however, will sometimes make it possible to add an important part and will also serve as a guide to the registration.
3. Pedal parts such as those in the Handel oratorios and Bach cantatas should be played non-legato, particularly when the part is taken from the *continuo* bass line, which outlines harmonic patterns.

The following examples illustrate some of the ways of adapting oratorio scores.

Handel

Mendelssohn

Brahms

The published "organ scores" of oratorio accompaniments are useful as guides to the inexperienced organist, but they represent only one approach to the technique of arranging and sometimes do not fit the situation which the organist faces, particularly in regard to the instrument being played. The organist should, as soon as possible, develop his own techniques in the art of arranging accompaniments in order to achieve the most artistic results.

# part eight

# Scales for Manuals and Pedal

# Practice Techniques

The Belgian organist and teacher Jacques Lemmens (1823–1881) is generally considered to be the founder of the modern French organ school. His most important contributions in the field of pedagogy were new principles of manual and pedal technique. His system of pedaling included extensive use of the heel, less crossing of the feet, closer coordination between the feet, and the avoidance of unnecessary motion.

1. Review the section on Pedal Technique (p. 121).
2. The following order is suggested for the first learning of the scales: B-flat, A, A-flat, G, E, C, E-flat, F, B, D, D-flat, G-flat.
3. Practice the preparatory exercises until the motion of each foot is firmly established and the ankles are completely flexible.
4. The pedaling is designed to allow the feet to move closely together and parallel. Keep the heels and toes touching the pedal keys.
5. Practice the scales with right hand and pedal, left hand and pedal, then both hands and pedal. Memorize the pedaling as well as the fingering.
6. Practice one-octave scales before beginning the two-octave scales.
7. Practice all scales in various ways, legato, non-legato, staccato, and with rhythms and articulations.
8. Start with a slow tempo and maintain this basic pulse for each group of scales until the rhythm patterns have been mastered.
9. When the left foot ascends into the upper octave of the pedal board, or the right foot descends into the lower octave, it may be necessary to reverse the position of the foot. The ankles should be kept turned in as long as possible.
10. Use clear, contrasting 8′ and 4′ stops for both manuals and pedal. Do not use 16′ pedal stops.
11. The daily practice of scales should continue throughout the career of the organist. The practice should always be meaningful and full of variety.

## C MAJOR

230

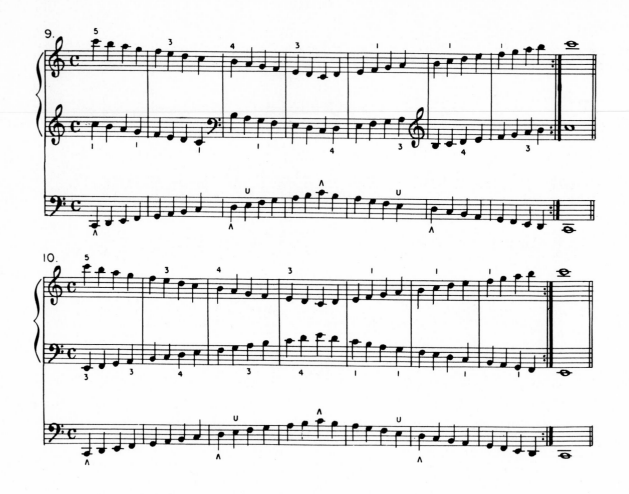

## G MAJOR

F MAJOR

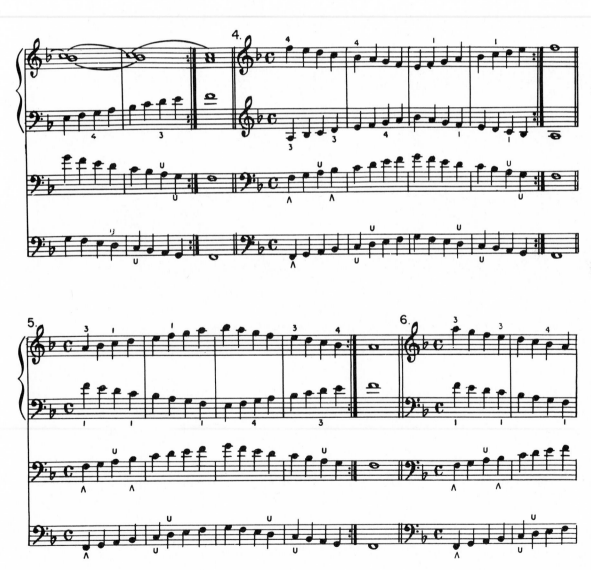

D MAJOR

## B-FLAT MAJOR

## E-FLAT MAJOR

## E MAJOR

248

249

A-FLAT MAJOR

# B MAJOR

**D-FLAT MAJOR**

256

**G-FLAT MAJOR**

## CHROMATIC SCALES

## MAJOR SCALES IN OCTAVES

## CHROMATIC SCALE IN OCTAVES

# Appendices

# Appendix A

## GRADED COURSE IN ORGAN PLAYING

Music may be selected from the following lists, or works of comparable difficulty and quality may be substituted.

### Organ I

Gleason: *Method of Organ Playing*
  Manual Technique
  Pedal Technique
  Compositions for Manuals
  Studies and Compositions for Manuals and Pedal
Bach: *Orgelbüchlein* (BWV 599–644)
  *Christ lag in Todesbanden*
  *Herr Christ der ein'ge Gottes Sohn*
  *Es ist das Heil*
  *Gelobet seist du, Jesu Christ*
  *Vater unser im Himmelreich*
  *Ich ruf' zu dir*
  *Herzlich thut mich verlangen* (*Method*, p. 212)
  *Fugue in G Minor* (BWV 578)
Frescobaldi: *Fiori Musicali:* Pieces selected from the *Messa delli Apostoli*
Buxtehude: *Prelude and Fugue in F Major* (Hansen, Vol. II, No. 18)
Brahms: Chorale Preludes
  *O Welt ich muss dich lassen* (two settings)
  *Es ist ein Ros' entsprungen*
  *Herzliebster Jesu*
  *O wie selig seid ihr doch, ihr Frommen*
Contemporary Compositions:
  Bornefeld: *Choralvorspiele* (Bärenreiter)
  Distler: *Dreissig Spielstücke* (Bärenreiter)
  Finney: *Five Fantasies, No. 4* (Peters)
  Kee: *Vier Manuaalstukken* (Donemus)
  Langlais: *Three Characteristic Pieces* (Novello)
  Messiaen: *Le Banquet Céleste* (Leduc)
  Pinkham: *4 Short Pieces for Manuals* (E. C. Schirmer)

### Organ II

Gleason: *Method of Organ Playing*
  Manual Technique
  Pedal Exercises and Scales
  Compositions for Manuals and Pedal
Bach: *Fantasie and Fugue in C Minor* (BWV 537)
  *Das alte Jahr vergangen ist* (BWV 614) (*Orgelbüchlein*)
  *In dir ist Freude* (BWV 615) (*Orgelbüchlein*)
Pachelbel: *Toccata in E Minor*
  *Partita: Was Gott tut, dass ist wohlgetan*
Sweelinck: *Puer nobis nascitur*
Reger: *30 Short Chorale Preludes* (Opus 135a)
Lübeck: *Praeambulum in E Major*
Brahms: Chorale Preludes
  *Herzlich thut mich verlangen* (two settings)
Dandrieu: *Noël pour l'amour de Marie*
  *Noël de Saintonge*
Buxtehude: *Präludium, Fuga und Ciacona*
  *Von Gott will ich nicht lassen*
  *Wie schön leuchtet der Morgenstern*
Reger: *Orgelstücke* (Opus 59, Heft II)
Couperin: *Messe pour les Couvents*
  *Chromhorne sur la Taille*
  *Offertoire sur les grands jeux*
Mendelssohn: *Sonata in C Minor* (No. II)
Cabezón: *Diferencias sobre el canto ilano del Caballero*
Brahms: Chorale Preludes
  *Schmücke dich, O liebe Seele*
  *Herzlich thut mich erfreuen*
Bach: *Trio Sonata, No. 1* (BWV 525)
  *Toccata and Fugue in D Minor* (BWV 565)
  *Wachet auf, ruft uns die Stimme* (BWV 645) (*Sechs Choräle*)
  *Meine Seele erhebt den Herren* (BWV 648) (*Sechs Choräle*)
  *Prelude and Fugue in B Minor* (BWV 544)
Du Mage: *Livre d'Orgue*
Franck: *Cantabile*
Contemporary Compositions:
  Ahrens: *Choralpartita über Lobe den Herren* (Schott)

Alain: Pieces from Vol. III  (Leduc)
Finney: *Five Fantasies,* No. 1, 2, 3, 5  (Peters)
Langlais: *Suite Médiévale*  (Salabert)
Messiaen: *Les Bergers*  (*La Nativité*)  (Leduc)
Pepping: Pieces from the *Kleines Orgelbuch* (Schott)
Persichetti: *Drop, Drop, Slow Tears*  (Elkan-Vogel)
Roberts: *Nova*  (Belwin-Mills)

### Organ III

Gleason: *Method of Organ Playing*
   Pedal Scales
   Broken Chords
   Advanced Exercises
Bach: *Trio Sonatas* No. 2  (BWV 526) and No. 4 (BWV 528)
   *O Mensch, bewein' dein' Sünde gross*  (BWV 622)  (*Orgelbüchlein*)
   *In dulci jubilo*  (BWV 608)  (*Orgelbüchlein*)
   *Wir glauben all' an einen Gott, Schöpfer*  (BWV 680)  (*Clavierübung* III)
d'Aquin: *Noëls*
Franck: *Prélude, Fugue and Variation*
Bach: *Prelude and Fugue in A minor*  (BWV 543)
Mendelssohn: *Sonatas* Nos. 6, 1
Bach: *Nun komm' der Heiden Heiland*  (BWV 659)  (*18 Great Chorales*)
   *Nun freut euch*  (BWV 734)
   *Schmücke dich, O liebe Seele*  (BWV 654)  (*18 Great Chorales*)
Clérambault: *Premier Livre d'Orgue*
Hindemith: *Sonata II*
Bach: *Partite diverse "O Gott du frommer Gott"*  (BWV 767)
Franck: *Pièce Héroïque*
Bach: *Prelude and Fugue in G Major*  (BWV 541)

### Contemporary Compositions:

Kee: *Reeks-Veranderingen I in 4 Secties*  (Donemus)
Langlais: *Hymne d'Actions de Grâces "Te Deum"*  (Philippo)
Lazarof: *Largo*  (Western International Music, Inc.)
   *Lamenti*
Messiaen: *Verset pour la Fête de la Dédicace*  (Leduc)
   *La Nativité: Les Anges*
              *Les Enfants de Dieu*
Pinkham: *A Prophecy*  (E. C. Schirmer)
   *When the Morning Stars Sang Together*  (organ and tape)

### Organ IV

Works selected from the following:
Bach: *Trio Sonatas,* No. 3  (BWV 527),  No. 5 (BWV 529), No. 6  (BWV 530)
   *Nun komm' der Heiden Heiland*  (BWV 661) (*18 Great Chorales*)
Franck: *Trois Chorals*  (A minor, B minor, E Major)
Distler: *Partita: Wachet auf, ruft uns die Stimme*
   *Partita: Nun komm' der Heiden Heiland*
Bach: *Fantasia and Fugue in G minor*  (BWV 542)
Hindemith: *Sonatas,* I, III
Alain: *Litanies*
   *Deuxième Fantaisie*
   *Trois Danses*
Bach: *Passacaglia*  (BWV 582)
Widor: Movements from the ten symphonies: No. 4 (Scherzo), No. 5 (Adagio, Toccata), No. 6 (Allegro, Adagio), No. 9 (*Gothique*), No. 10 (*Romane*)
Martin: *Passacaglia*
Dupré: *Trois Préludes et Fugues,* Op. 7
Bach: *Toccata, Adagio and Fugue in C Major*  (BWV 564)
Vierne: Movements from the six symphonies: No. 1 (Prelude, Final), No. 2 (*Scherzo*), No. 5 (*Final*), No. 6
Grigny: *Livre d'Orgue*
Tournemire: *L'Orgue Mystique:* Nos. 3, 7, 11, 35
Reubke: *Sonata on the Ninety-fourth Psalm*
Langlais: *Cinq Méditations sur l'Apocalypse*
Bach: *Prelude and Fugue in E-flat*  (BWV 552)
Reger: *Phantasie über den Choral Halleluja! Gott zu Loben,* Op. 52/53
   *Fantasie und Fuge,* Op. 135
Roger-Ducasse: *Pastorale*
Sowerby: *Suite*
   *Symphony in G Major*
Duruflé: *Prélude, Adagio et Choral varié, "Veni, creator"*
Bach: *Toccata in F Major*  (BWV 540)
Messiaen: *Messe de la Pentecôte*
   *Méditations sur le Mystère de la Sainte Trinité*

### Additional Contemporary Compositions:

Berlinski: "And Behold the Bush Burneth"  (Belwin-Mills)
Albright: *Juba*  (Elkan-Vogel)
   *Organbook I* and *II*  (Jobert)
Cooper: *Variants*  (Chester/Hansen)
Camilleri: *Invocation to the Creator*  (Roberton)
Eder: *Vox Media*  (Doblinger)

Felciano: *I Make My Own Soul . . .* (Organ and tape) (E. C. Schirmer)

Guillou: *Dix-huit Variations* (Leduc)
  *Toccata*
  *Sinfonietta*
  *Sagas*

Mellnäs: *Fixations* (Peters)

Diemente: *Diary (Part I 1972)* (Seesaw)

Ligeti: *Zwei Etüden für Orgel* (Schott)
  *Volumina* (Peters)

Sifler: *The Despair and Agony of Dachau* (Belwin-Mills)

Persichetti: *Shimah B'koli* (Elkan-Vogel)
  *Parable*
  *Do Not Go Gentle* (Pedals Alone)

Works for organ and instruments and organ concertos by Adler, Barber, Bolcom, Casella, Dupré, Felciano, Guillou, Handel, Hanson, Haydn, Heiller, Hovhaness, Jongen, Langlais, Lockwood, Mozart, Peeters, Pinkham, Piston, Poulenc, Sowerby.

# Appendix B

## ORGAN SPECIFICATIONS

The following specifications include organs which are associated with many outstanding organ composers, and they are representative of various periods, countries, and organ builders. The original specifications of many organs are rarely available and other specifications often represent numerous rebuildings and restorations which do not always agree in details.

| | | |
|---|---|---|
| I | Arnolt Schlick (Germany) | 1511 |
| II | Évora Cathedral (Portugal) | 1562 |
| III | Oude Kerk, Amsterdam | 1567 |
| IV | Cathedral of Brescia | 1536 |
| V | San Martino of Bologna | 1556 |
| VI | St. George's Church, Rötha | 1721 |
| VII | Totentanzorgel (Marienkirche), Lübeck | 1621 |
| VIII | Moritzkirche, Halle | 1624 |
| IX | St. Peter's Church, Cornhill (London) | 1840 |
| X | Saint-Gervais, Paris | 1684 |
| XI | Jakobikirche, Hamburg | 1721 |
| XII | St. Paul's Cathedral, London | 1695–1800–1826–1849 |
| XIII | Neuekirche (Bonifatiuskirche), Arnstadt | 1701 |
| XIV | Hauptkirche Divi Blasii, Mühlhausen | 1708 |
| XV | Schlosskirche, Weimar | 1714 |
| XVI | Thomaskirche, Leipzig | 1721 |
| XVII | Frauenkirche, Dresden | 1732 |
| XVIII | Handel's Organ for Charles Jennens | 1749 |
| XIX | Sainte-Clotilde, Paris | 1859 |
| XX | Church of the Immaculate Conception, Boston | 1863 |
| XXI | First United Methodist Church, Pasadena | 1924 |
| XXII | Strong Auditorium, University of Rochester | 1937 |
| XXIII | Memorial Church, Harvard University | 1967 |
| XXIV | Lawrence Phelps | 1977 |

The specifications are based on the study of a considerable number of different sources, including original documents.

## SPECIFICATION I

### Arnolt Schlick (Germany)

Arnolt Schlick (c. 1540–c. 1525), in his *Spiegel der Orgelmacher*, 1511, describes sample specifications for two organs, one "small" and one "large." The small organ is based on the 8′ Principal pitch; the large one, based on 16′ pitch, is about the same size but requires a larger case. The registers in parentheses are included in the large organ. The stop-list is in modern spelling.

### Hauptwerk (F-a², 41 notes)

(Principal 2 rks.   16')    Gemshorn   4'          Rauschpfeif = Krummhorn   8'
Principal 2 rks.   8'       (Schwegel = Flute   2')    Zinck   8'
Octave   4'
Hintersatz 16–18 rks.
Zimbel

### Rückpositiv (F-a², 41 notes)

(Principal   8')           (Gemshorn   4')
Principal   4'             Gemshorn   2'
Hintersatz, Small         *Hülze glechter*
Zimbel

### (Brustwerk?)

(Regal   8')

Schlick considered more than two manuals "much sauce with little fish."

### Pedal (F-c', 20 notes)

Principal   8' (16')    Trompete   8'
Octave   4' (8')        (or Posaune)
Hintersatz

The *Hülze glechter* (wooden laughter) was described by Schlick as "rare and wonderful," but sounded "as if young boys were playing on a pot with spoons." It may have been a xylophone, or a noisy tremulant.

## SPECIFICATION II

### *Évora Cathedral (Portugal)*

This organ was built c. 1562 by an unknown builder. The Italian builder Caetano made changes c. 1760, and the horizontal reeds were added c. 1800, but the builder Dirk Flentrop and Dr. Maarten Vente, who restored the instrument in 1966–1969, believed that much of the original instrument had remained intact. It is suitable for the music of Manuel Rodriguez Coelho (c. 1555–1635), Cabezón, Correa de Arauxo, and other early Spanish and Portuguese composers.

### Manual (FGA-g²a², or FGA-c³) (39 or 42 notes)

Flautado (Principal)   (C, D, E, F, B-flat are 8')    16'
Flautado (Principal)   8'
Vos humana   (A treble principal tuned flat to Flautado   8'
   to be used like the Italian Piffaro)   8'
Flauta da pão da mano esquierda   (Flute, bass only)   8'
Corneta de 4 por punto   (Cornet 4 rks. treble only)   4', 2⅔', 2', 1⅗'
Outava real   (Octave 4')   4'
Quinta real   (12th)   2⅔'
Decimaquinta y decimasetima   (Octave and Tierce)   2⅔', 1⅗'
Cheio de Registros   (Mixture, 4 rks.)   1⅓'
Tamborhen   (Drum)   (2 pipes 8' open, tuned to A and B)

**Pedal**

Six pedal pull-downs (C, D, E, F, G, A)
  Manual (c. 1800)
Two horizontal Reeds
  Trompeta real da mano esquierda (Bass only)   8'
  Clarim da mano direita (Treble only)   8'


# SPECIFICATION III

### Oude Kerk, Amsterdam

The large organ in the Old Church was built by Hendrik Niehoff, Herman Niehoff, and Hans Suys of Cologne in 1539–1542. It was restored by Peter Jansz in 1567 (1558?). Sweelinck played this organ from 1580 until his death in 1621.

## Grote Orgel
### Bovenwerk (upper manual) (C-a²)

| | | |
|---|---|---|
| Doeff (Principal)  8' | Holpyep  8' | Synck (Zink)  8' |
| Rusent Zymbel (Terzimbel) | Oepen floyt  4' | Trompet  8' |
| | Asaet (Nazard)  2⅔' | |
| | Gemsenhoorn  2' | |
| | Sufflet  1⅓' | |

### Hoofdwerk (middle manual) (F-a²)

Groete Doeff   16'
Octaeff   8' + 4'
Mycxtuer
Scherp

### Rugwerk (lower manual) (F-a²)

| | | |
|---|---|---|
| Doeff  8' | Quyntedeen  8' | Baerpijp (regal)  8' |
| Octaeff  4' | Holpyep  4' | Schalmei  4' |
| Mycxtuer | Sufflet  1⅓' | |
| Scherp | | |

### Pedal (F-c¹)

| | |
|---|---|
| Nachthoorn  2' | Trompet  8' |

The pedal stops extended from c-c¹. Through the coupler HW/Ped. the compass extended to F.

In 1544 the Nazard replaced a Quintadena on the Bovenwerk and the Sifflet replaced a Kromhoorn on the Rugwerk.


# SPECIFICATION IV

### Cathedral of Brescia (The Old Cathedral, S. Maria Rotonda)

The specification of the organ built by Gian Giacomo Antegnati in 1536 is given by Costanzo Antegnati in his *L'Arte Organica* (1608). The stops are numbered by Antegnati from one to twelve and named according to their pitch relation to the *Principale*. The pitch of the *Principale* is not stated.

Principale  (through the entire compass)
Principale spezzato  (a divided stop, played on the manual in the treble and on the pedal in the bass, below tenor d)
Ottava  (Octave)
Quintadecima  (Fifteenth)
Decimanona  (Nineteenth)
Vigesimaseconda  (Twenty-second)
Vigesimasesta  (Twenty-sixth)
Vigesimanona  (Twenty-ninth)
Trigesimaterza  (Thirty-third)
Un'altra Vigesimaseconda  (another Twenty-second to combine with the Octave, the Flute octave and the Nineteenth to imitate *cornetti*)
Flauto in quintadecima  (Flute fifteenth)
Flauto in ottava  (Flute octave)
(Tremulant?)

## SPECIFICATION V

### San Martino of Bologna

This organ was built by Giovanni Cipri in 1556. It is one of the best preserved organs in Italy, and the stop-list is the original one. The organ is an 8′ organ, with a compass of four octaves, the lower octave being a "short" octave. However, there is an added lower octave which couples to the pedal, giving the pedal independent 16′ pitches. The pedalboard contains eighteen keys.

Principale  8′
Ottava  4′
Quintadecima  2′
Decimanona  $1\frac{1}{3}$′
Vigesimaseconda  1′
Vigesimasesta  $\frac{2}{3}$′
Vigesimanona  $\frac{1}{2}$′
Trigesimaterza  $\frac{1}{3}$′
Flauto in ottava  4′
Flauto in duodecima  $2\frac{2}{3}$′
Voce Umana  8′ (16′)

The stops from the Principale through the $\frac{1}{3}$′ form the *Ripieno*.

## SPECIFICATION VI

### St. George's Church, Rötha

This organ was built by Gottfried Silbermann in 1718–1721. It is one that Mendelssohn praised highly and played often. Rötha is near Leipzig.

### Hauptwerk (C-c³, without low C♯)

| | |
|---|---|
| Principal  8′ | Bourdon  16' |
| Octave  4′ | Rohrflöte  8′ |
| Quinta  3′ | Spitzflöte  4′ |
| Octave  2′ | |
| Mixtur 3 rks.  $1\frac{1}{2}$′ | |
| Cymbel 2 rks.  1′ | |
| Cornet 3 rks. | |

### Oberwerk (C-c³ without low C♯)

| | |
|---|---|
| Principal 4′ | Gedakt 8′ |
| Nasat 3′ | Quintaden 8′ |
| Octave 2′ | Rohrflöte 4′ |
| Mixtur 3 rks. | Nasat 3′ |
| | Tertia 1⅗′ |
| | Quinta 1½′ |
| | Sufflet 1′ |

### Pedal (C-c¹ without low C♯)

| | |
|---|---|
| Principalbass 16′ | Posaune 16′ |
| | Trompete 8′ |

Tremulant—Manualschiebekoppel—2 Sperrventile—HW/Ped., OW/HW

# SPECIFICATION VII

### *Totentanzorgel (Marienkirche), Lübeck*

This organ dates from 1475–1557–1621. It was played by Bach when he was with Buxtehude (October, 1705–February, 1706).

### Brustwerk (upper manual)

Added by Henning Kroeger, Wismar, in 1621–1622

| | |
|---|---|
| Gedackt 8′ | Krummhorn 8′ |
| Quintade 4′ | Schalmei 4′ |
| Hohlflöte 2′ | |
| Quintflöte 1⅓′ | |
| Scharff 4 rks. | |

### Hauptwerk (middle manual), 1475-1477

| | | |
|---|---|---|
| Prinzipal 8′ | Quintade 16′ | Trompete 8′ |
| (in front) | Spitzflöte 8′ | |
| Oktave 4′ | Nasat 2⅔′ | |
| Mixture 8-10 rks. | Rauschpfeife 2 rks. | |

### Rückpositiv (lower manual)

Added by Jacob Scherer, Hamburg, in 1557–1558

| | | |
|---|---|---|
| Prinzipal 8′ | Quintade 8′ | Dulzian 16′ |
| (in front) | Rohrflöte 8′ | Trichterregal 8′ |
| Oktave 4′ | Rohrflöte 4′ | |
| Scharff 6-8 rks. | Sesquialtera 2 rks. | |
| | Sifflöte 1⅓′ | |

### Pedal (1475-1477, 1621-1622)

| | | |
|---|---|---|
| Prinzipal 16′ | Subbass 16′ | Posaune 16′ |
| (in front) | Gedackt 8′ | Trompete 8′ |
| Oktave 8′ | Quintade 4′ | Cornett 2′ |
| Oktave 4′ | | |
| Oktave 2′ | | |
| Mixtur 4 rks. | Tremulant—Coupler: | |
| Zimbel 2 rks ′ | Rückpositiv to Hauptwerk. | |

## SPECIFICATION VIII

### *Moritzkirche, Halle*

The organ was built by Heinrich Compenius in 1624 under the direction of Samuel Scheidt (1587–1654).

### Hauptwerk (Oberwerk)

| | | |
|---|---|---|
| Prinzipal 8' | Quintadena 16' | Regal 8' |
| Oktav 4' | Gedackt 8' | |
| Sedetz (Oktav) 2' | Gedackt 4' | |
| Mixtur | Quinte 3' | |
| Zimbel | | |

### Rückpositiv

| | | |
|---|---|---|
| Prinzipal 4' | Grobgedackt 8' | Dulzian 8' |
| Sedetz 2' | Kleingedackt 4' | Regal 8' |
| | Spitzflöte 2' | Singend Regal 4' |
| | Quinte 1⅓' | |
| | Sifflöte 1' | |
| | Zimbel | |

### Pedal

| | |
|---|---|
| Subbass 16' | Posaune 16' |
| Quintadena 16' | (Dulzian 16'?) |
| Zimbelbass 2' | Dulzian 8' |
| Flötenbass 1' | Posaune 8' |
| | Kornett 4' |
| | (Kornett 2'?) |

Tremulant—Vogelgesang—Zimbelstern—Trommel—Kalkantenglocke—Sperrventils (Ped., Hw, Rp).

## SPECIFICATION IX

### *St. Peter's Church, Cornhill (London)*

This organ, built by William Hill in 1840, was one that Mendelssohn particularly enjoyed playing. It had many divided stops, controlled by two stop-knobs.

### Grand Organ (C-f³)

| | |
|---|---|
| Tenoroon diapason to c 16' | Stopped flute 4' |
| Bourdon from c 16' | Twelfth 2⅔' |
| Principal diapason 8' | Fifteenth 2' |
| Stopped diapason treble 8' | Tierce 1⅗' |
| Stopped diapason bass 8' | Sesquialtera 3 rks. |
| Dulciana to c 8' | Mixture 2 rks. |
| Claribel flute to c 8' | Doublette 2 rks. |
| Principal octave 4' | Corno trombone 8' |
| Wald flute 4' | Corno clarion 4' |
| Oboe flute 4' | Cromorne to c 8' |

## Swell Organ (C-f³)

| | | | |
|---|---|---|---|
| Tenoroon dulciana to c | 16′ | Fifteenth | 2′ |
| Bourdon from c | 16′ | Piccolo to c | 2′ |
| Principal diapason | 8′ | Sesquialtera | 3 rks. |
| Stopped diapason treble | 8′ | Mixture | 2 rks. |
| Stopped diapason bass | 8′ | Echo dulciana cornet | 5 rks. |
| Principal octave | 4′ | Cornopean | 8′ |
| Suabe flute to c | 4′ | Tromba | 8′ |
| Flageolet to c | 4′ | Oboe | 8′ |
| Twelfth | 2⅔′ | Clarion | 4′ |

## Pedal (CC-d¹)

Grand diapason   16′
Grand trombone   16′
Pedal stops only on the bottom octave

Couplers: SW/Gr; Gr/Ped; Sw/Ped; Oct/Ped/; 4 Composition pedals.


# SPECIFICATION X

### Saint-Gervais, Paris

Pierre Thierry built an organ for St. Gervais in 1649 which was rebuilt in 1659. It was rebuilt by Alexandre Thierry in 1684 with the specification given below. Members of the famous family of Couperin were organists at St. Gervais from 1650 until 1826. François Couperin (1668–1773) was the organist from 1685 until his death, and he registered his two Organ Masses (1690) for this instrument.

### Quatrième Clavier (c¹-c³)

Cornet séparé

### Troisième Clavier: Echo (c¹-c³)

| | |
|---|---|
| Cornet | Cromorne   (8′) |
| Cymbale | |

### Deuxième Clavier: Grand Orgue (A, C, D-c³) (C♯ key played the A)

| | | | | | |
|---|---|---|---|---|---|
| Montre | 16′ | Bourdon | 16′ | Trompette | (8′) |
| Montre | 8′ | Bourdon | 8′ | Clairon | (4′) |
| Prestant | (4′) | Flûte | 4′ | Voix humaine | (8′) |
| Doublette | (2′) | Grosse Tierce | (3⅕′) | | |
| Fourniture | 3 rks. | Nazard | (2⅔′) | | |
| Cymbale | 3 rks. | Tierce | (1⅗′) | | |
| | | Cornet | (c¹-c³) | | |

### Premier Clavier: Positif (A-C-D-c³) (C♯ key played A)

| | | | | | |
|---|---|---|---|---|---|
| Montre | 4′ | Bourdon | 8′ | Cromorne | (8′) |
| Doublette | (2′) | Flûte | 4′ | | |
| Fourniture | 3 rks. | Nazard | (2⅔′) | | |
| Cymbale | 3 rks. | Tierce | (1⅗′) | | |
| | | Larigot | (1⅓′) | | |

## Pédale (A, C, D-e[1])

| | |
|---|---|
| Flûte 8′ | Trompette (8′) |
| Flûte 4′ | |

Couplers: G.O./Pos.; G.O./Péd.

# SPECIFICATION XI

### *Jakobikirche, Hamburg*

The first significant organ, built in 1512, had one manual and pedal. It was rebuilt and enlarged several times, and in 1688–1693 it was completely rebuilt by Arp Schnitger. Bach sought, but failed to get, an appointment as organist at St. Jakobikirche in 1720. The following specification was printed by Johann Mattheson in 1721.

### Brust (upper manual)

| | | |
|---|---|---|
| Principal 8′ | Hohlflöte 4′ | Dulcian 8′ |
| Octava 4′ | Waldflöte 2′ | Trichter-Regal 8′ |
| Scharff 5 rks. | Sesquialtera 2 rks. | |

### Oberwerk (third manual)

| | | |
|---|---|---|
| Principal (8′) | Rohrflöte 8′ | Krummhorn 8′ |
| Octava 4′ | Holtzflöte 8′ | Trommete 8′ |
| Nasat 3′ | Spitzflöte 4′ | Trommete 4′ |
| Octava 2′ | Gemshorn 2′ | |
| Mixtura 6 rks. | | |
| Cimbel 3 rks. | | |

### Hauptwerk (second manual)

| | | |
|---|---|---|
| Principal 16′ | Quintadena 16′ | Trommete 16′ |
| Octava 8′ | Spitzflöte 8′ | |
| Octava 4′ | Rohrflöte 4′ | |
| Super-Octava 2′ | Blockflöte 2′ | |
| Mixtura 6 rks. | Rauschflöte 2 rks. | |
| | Gedact im Cammerton 8′ | |

### Rückpositiv (lower manual)

| | | |
|---|---|---|
| Principal 8′ | Gedact 8′ | Dulcian 16′ |
| Octava 4′ | Quintadena 8′ | Baarpfeiffe 8′ |
| Scharff 4-5-6 rks. | Querflöte 4′ | Schallmey 4′ |
| | Floete 4′ | |
| | Blockflöte 2′ | |
| | Sifflet 1½′ | |
| | Sesquialtera 2 rks. | |

### Pedal

| | | |
|---|---|---|
| Principal 32′ | Subbass 16′ | Posaune 32′ |
| Octava 16′ | Nachthorn 2′ | Posaune 16′ |
| Octava 8′ | Rauschpfeiffe 2 rks. | Dulcian 16′ |
| Octava 4′ | (2′, 1⅓′) | Trommete 8′ |
| Mixtura 6 rks. | | Trommete 4′ |
| | | Cornet 2′ |

Tremulants: Oberwerk and Rückpositiv—Couplers: Oberwerk to Hauptwerk; Brust to Oberwerk—Cimbel Sterne.


## SPECIFICATION XII

### St. Paul's Cathedral, London

"Father" Bernard Smith built a new organ for St. Paul's Cathedral in 1695–1696. His successor, Christopher Shrider, enlarged the organ in 1720. He added toe-pedals, which pulled down the lower notes of the Great, and a swell box which would open and close for the "Echoes or halfe Stops." He also added "six large Trumpet Pipes down to 16 Foot Tone to be used with a Pedal or without" (the first recorded use of pedals in England). The organ was rebuilt in 1800 by John Crang and others, and in 1826 and 1849 by J. C. Bishop.

Maurice Greene (1695–1755) was organist at St. Paul's from 1718 to 1755 and, according to Burney, Handel often played the organ there "for the exercise it afforded him in the use of the pedals." Mendelssohn (1809–1847) came to England many times after his first visit in 1829, and there are accounts of his performances on the organ at St. Paul's. His *Six Organ Sonatas* were published in London in 1845.

| 1695-1696 Great Organ | 1800 Great Organ (C-c³) (no C♯) | 1826 Great Organ (cc-f³) |
|---|---|---|
| (Father Smith) | (John Crang and others) | (J. C. Bishop) |
| Open Diapason | Open Diapason (East) | Open Diapason (East) |
| Open Diapason | Open Diapason (West) | Open Diapason (West) |
| Stop Diapason | Stopped Diapason | Stopped Diapason (Clarabella treble) |
| Principall | Principal | Principal |
| Great Twelfth | Twelfth | Twelfth |
| fifteenth | Fifteenth | Fifteenth |
| | Block flute | Block flute |
| Small Twelfth | Tierce | Tierce |
| Cornet | Cornet  5 rks. | Trumpet (to middle C) |
| Mixtures | Mixture  3 rks. | Mixture  3 rks. |
| Sesquialtera | Sesquialtera  4 rks. | Sesquialtera  4 rks. |
| Trumpet | Trumpet | Trumpet |
| Hol fleut | Nason | Clarion |

| Chayre Organ | Choir Organ (F-c³) (no F♯ or G♯) | Choir Organ (FF-f³) |
|---|---|---|
| Principall | Principal | Principal |
| Stop Diapason | Stopped Diapason | Stopped Diapason |
| Hol fleut | Flute | Flute |
| Voice Humane | Vox Humana | Dulciana |
| Crum horne | Cremona | Cremona |
| Great Twelfth | Twelfth | Twelfth |
| Fifteenth | Fifteenth | Fifteenth |
| Quinta Dena Diapason | | |
| Cimball | Mixture  3 rks. | Open Diapason |

| "Echoes or halfe Stops" | Swell Organ (G-f³) | Swell Organ (G-f³) |
|---|---|---|
| Diapason | Open Diapason | Open Diapason |
| Principall | Principal | Principal |
| Cornet | Cornet 3 rks. | Cornet 3 rks. |
| Trumpet | Trumpet | Trumpet |
| Fifteenth | Hautboy | Hautboy |
| Nason | Stopped Diapason | Stopped Diapason |

| Pedal | Pedal | Pedal (CC-c') |
|---|---|---|
| No pedal pipes. Two octaves of toe pedals to pull down the manual keys. | | Pedal 16' (one octave). Toe pedals replaced by German type pedals. |

Four composition pedals—Sw./Gt.; Sw./Ped.; Gt./Ped.; Ch./Ped.

## SPECIFICATION XIII

### *Neuekirche (Bonifatiuskirche), Arnstadt*

Built by Johann Friedrich Wender of Mühlhausen in 1701–1703. Bach was the organist from 1703–1707.

#### Brustwerk (upper manual)

| Prinzipal 4' | Gedackt 8' |
|---|---|
| Mixtur 4 rks. | Nachthorn 4' |
| | Quinte 3' |
| | Spitzflöte 2' |
| | Sesquialtera |

#### Oberwerk (lower manual)

| Prinzipal 8' | Quintadena 8' | Trompete 8' |
|---|---|---|
| Oktave 4' | Gedackt 8' | |
| Mixtur 4 rks. | Viola de Gamba 8' | |
| Zimbel (Scharf) 3 rks. | Gemshorn 8' | |
| | Quinte 6' | |

#### Pedal

| Violon-Bass 16' | Subbass 16' | Posaune 16' |
|---|---|---|
| Oktave 8' | | |
| Hohlflöte 4' | | |

Manual Coupler; OW/Ped.—Cymbelstern—Tremulant to Oberwerk

## SPECIFICATION XIV

### *Hauptkirche Divi Blasii, Mühlhausen*

Bach was organist of the Church of St. Blasius from June, 1707, to June, 1708. The organ was rebuilt to Bach's specification by Johann F. Wender in 1708–1709. The Brustwerk was entirely new and an Untersatz 32' and a Glockenspiel were added to the pedal. In the Oberwerk, the Gemshorn was replaced by a Viol di Gamba 8', the Trumpet (8') by a Fagotto 16', and the Quinta 3' by a Nassat 3'. Bach's original spelling has been retained for the new stops and for the "Salicinal." The compass of the manuals was C, D-d³ and of the pedals, C, D-d¹.

### Brustwerk (upper manual)

| | | |
|---|---|---|
| Stillgedackt (wood)  8' | Schalemoy (in front)  8' | |
| Fleute douce  4' | (Schalmei) | |
| Principal  2' | | |
| Tertia  (1⅗') | | |
| Quinte  ⅓' | | |
| Mixture  3 rks. | | |

### Oberwerk [Hauptwerk] (middle manual)

| | | |
|---|---|---|
| Principal  8' | Quintatön  16' | Fagotto  16' |
| Oktave  4' | Viol di Gamba  8' | |
| Oktave  2' | Gedackt  4' | |
| Mixtur  4 rks. | Nassat (2⅔')  3' | |
| Cymbel  2 rks. | Sesquialtera  2 rks. | |

### Rückpositiv (lower manual)

| | |
|---|---|
| Principal  4' | Quintatöon  8' |
| Oktave  2' | Gedackt  8' |
| Cymbel  3 rks. | Salicinal  4' |
| | Sesquialtera  2 rks. |
| | Spitzflöte  2' |
| | Quintflöte  1⅓' |

### Pedal

| | | |
|---|---|---|
| Untersatz  32' | Sub-Bass  16' | Posaune  16' |
| Principal  16' | Rohrflöte  1' | Trompete  8', |
| Oktave  8' | Glockenspiel | Kornett  2' |
| Oktave  4' | (26 bells at 4' pitch) | |
| Mixture  4 rks. | | |

Couplers: BW/OW; RP/OW; OW/Ped.—Tremulant to all 3 manuals—Zimbelstern-Pauke

## SPECIFICATION XV

### Schlosskirche, Weimar

Bach was the court organist and chamber musician to the Duke of Weimar from 1708–1717. He composed many of his great organ works during this period. This organ was built by Ludwig Compenius in 1658, rebuilt in 1707–1708 and 1714.

### Oberwerk (upper manual)

| | |
|---|---|
| Quintadena  16' | Gemshorn  8' |
| Principal  8' | Grobgedackt  8' |
| Octave  4' | Quintadena  4' |
| Mixture  6 rks. | |
| Cymbel  3 rks. | |
| A Glockenspiel and | |
| a stop knob for it. | |

### Unterwerk (lower manual)

| | | |
|---|---|---|
| Principal 8′ | Viol da Gamba 8′ | Trompette 8′ |
| Octave 4′ | Gedackt 8′ | |
| | Klein Gedackt 4′ | |
| | Wald-Flöthe 2′ | |
| | Sesquialtera 2 rks. | |

### Pedal

| | | |
|---|---|---|
| Gross Untersatz (wood) 32′ | Sub-bass 16′ | Posaune-bass 16′ |
| Violon-bass 16′ | | Trompeten-bass 8′ |
| Principal-bass 8′ | | Cornetten-bass 4′ |

Tremulants to Oberwerk and Unterwerk—Couplers: manual to pedal, manual to manual—Cymbelstern.

## SPECIFICATION XVI

### *Thomaskirche, Leipzig*

The first organ was built in 1489 and repaired in 1590. It was rebuilt in 1721–1722 by Johann Scheibe of Leipzig. Bach was Cantor and *Director Musices* at St. Thomas's from 1723 until his death.

### Brustwerk (upper manual)

| | | |
|---|---|---|
| Prinzipal 4′ | Gedackt 8′ | Regal 8′ |
| Zimbel 2 rks. | Nachthorn 4′ | Geigenregal 4′ |
| | Nassat 3′ | |
| | Gemshorn 2′ | |
| | Sesquialtera | |

### Hauptwerk (middle manual)

| | |
|---|---|
| Prinzipal 16′ | Quintadena 8′ |
| Oktave 8′ | Spillflöte 8′ |
| Oktave 4′ | Sesquialtera 2 rks. |
| Quinte 3′ | |
| Oktave 2′ | |
| Mixtur 6-8-10 rks. | |

### Rückpositiv (lower manual)

| | | |
|---|---|---|
| Prinzipal 8′ | Quintadena 8′ | Krummhorn 16′ |
| Oktave (conical) 4′ | Gedackt 8′ | Trompete 8′ |
| Violine (Oktave) 2′ | Gedackt 4′ | |
| Mixtur 4 rks. | Querflöte 4′ | |
| | Rauschpfeife 2 rks. | |
| | Waldflöte (1⅓′?) 2′ | |

### Pedal

| | |
|---|---|
| Subbass (metal) 16′ | Posaune 16′ |
| | Trompete 8′ |
| | Schalmei 4 |
| | Kornett 2′ |

Vogelgesang—Zimbelstern—Tremulant—Manual couplers—Coupler to Pedal

## SPECIFICATION XVII

*Frauenkirche, Dresden*

The *Dresdener Nachrichten* reported that "on December 1, 1736, the famous Mr. Bach played on the new organ in the Frauen Kirche. Among those present was the Russian Ambassador, Von Keyserlingk, many persons of rank, also a large attendance of other persons and artists." The organ was built by Gottfried Silbermann during the years 1732–1736.

### Oberwerk (upper manual; C, D-d³)

Principal 8'
  ("sharp and lovely")
Octava 4'
Octaven 2'
Nassat 3'
Mixtura 4 rks.

Quintaden 16'
Quintaden 8'
Gedackt 8'
Flöthen 4'
Sesquialtera 2 rks.
  ("through the entire
  compass")

Vox Humana 8'
  ("a beautiful reed
  perfectly imitat-
  ing the human
  voice")

### Hauptwerk (middle manual; C, D-d³)

Principal 16'
Octav-Principal 8'
Octava scharff 4'
Quinta 3'
Super-Octava 2'
Tertia 1⅗'
Mixtura 6 rks.
Cymbel 3 rks.

Viol di Gamba 8'
  (conical)
Rohr-Flöthen 8'
Spitzflöthe 4'
Cornetti 5 rks.

Fagott 16'
  ("beautiful and
  wonderful reed")
Trompeta 8'

### Brustwerk (lower manual; C, D-d³)

Principal 4'
  ("very sharp and
  brilliant")
Octava 2'
Quinta scharff 3'
Sifflet (Oktave) 1'
Mixtura 3 rks.

Gedackt 8'
Rohrflöte 4'
Nassat 3'
Gemshorn (Spitzflöte) 2'
  ("a very pleasing voice")

Chalumeau 8'
  ("a very pleasant
  sounding reed")

### Pedal (C, D-d¹)

Grosser Untersatz 32'
Principal-Bass 16'
Octav-Bass 8'
Octav-Bass 4'
Mixture 6 rks.
  (stately, strong and
sharp)

Posaunen-Bass 16'
Trompeten-Bass 8'
Clairon-Bass 4'

Coupler for HW—Bass ventil—Tremulant for HW and Pedal—Schwebung—Tuned in Kammerton

## SPECIFICATION XVIII

### Handel's Organ for Charles Jennens

This organ was designed by Handel in September of 1749, for Charles Jennens, his librettist. The organ was installed in Jennens's house at Gopsal in Leicestershire.

| | |
|---|---|
| An Open Diapason | of Metal throughout to be in Front. |
| A Stopt Diapason | the Treble Metal and the Bass Wood. |
| A Principal | of Metal throughout. |
| A Twelfth | of Metal throughout. |
| A Fifteenth | of Metal throughout. |
| A Great Tierce | of Metal throughout. |
| A Flute Stop | such a one is in Freeman's Organ. |

Handel wrote to Jennens: "I hereunder specify my Opinion of an Organ which I think will answer the Ends you propose, being every thing that is necessary for a good and grand Organ, without reed Stops, which I have omitted, because they are continually wanting to be tuned. . . . The Compass to be up to D and down to Gamut, full Octave, Church Work, one Row of Keys, whole Stops and none in halves."

## SPECIFICATION XIX

### Sainte-Clotilde, Paris

César Franck was the organist of Sainte-Clotilde from 1859 until 1890, and his compositions were registered for this instrument. The organ was built by Aristide Cavaillé-Coll in 1859. The following specification was given by Jean Langlais in a letter.

**Grand Orgue (C-f³)**

Montre   16'
Bourdon   16'
Montre   8'
Bourdon   8'
Flûte harmonique   8'
Viole de Gambe   8'
Prestant   4'
Ventil      Octave   4'
division   Quint   2⅔'
           Doublette   2'
           Plein Jeu harmonique
              7 rks.
           Bombarde   16'
           Trompette   8'
           Clairon   4'

**Positif (C-f³)**

Bourdon   16'
Montre   8'
Bourdon   8'
Flûte harmonique   8'
Gambe   8'
Unda Maris   8'
Prestant   4'

ELLISON, ROSS W. "Baroque Organ Registration, Chapter Eight of J. Adlung's *Musica Mechanica Organoedi*, 1768." Translation. *MUSIC (A.G.O.)*, (Jan. 1974), p. 25.

EMERY, WALTER. "On the Registration of Bach's Organ Preludes and Fugues." *Musical Times*, no. 1432 (1962), p. 396; no. 1433 (1962), p. 467.

FISKE, ROGER. "Handel's Organ Concertos—Do They Belong to Particular Oratorios?" *The Organ Yearbook* (1972), p. 14.

FLENTROP, DIRK A. "Organ Building in Europe." *The Diapason* (Nov. 1956), p. 22; (Dec. 1956), p. 8.

GLEASON, HAROLD. "A Seventeenth-Century Organ Instruction Book." *BACH* (Jan. 1972), p. 3.

GOMBOSI, OTTO. "About Organ Playing in the Divine Service, circa 1500." In *Essays on Music in Honor of A. T. Davison*. Cambridge: Harvard University Press, 1957, 51.

GOTWALS, VERNON. "Brahms and the Organ." *MUSIC (A.G.O.)*, (April 1970), p. 38.

GRAAF, G. A. C. DE. "A Spanish Registration List of 1789." *The Organ Yearbook* (1976), p. 76.

GUENTHER, EILEEN. "Composers of French Noël Variations in the 17th and 18th Centuries." *The Diapason*, (Dec. 1973), p. 1; (Jan. 1974), p. 1; (Feb. 1974), p. 4.

HANKS, SARAH. "The Organ Concerto Arrangements of Johann Gottfried Walther." *The Diapason* (Nov. 1974), p. 5; (Dec. 1974), p. 10.

HANTZ, EDWIN. "An Introduction to the Organ Music of William Albright," *The Diapason* (May 1973), p. 1.

HARMON, THOMAS. "The Mühlhausen Organ Revisited." *BACH*, (Jan. 1973), p. 3.
　　 "Performance and the *Affektenlehre* in Bach's *Orgelbuechlein*." *The Diapason* (Dec. 1972), p. 4; (April 1973), p. 4.
　　 "The Performance of Mozart's Church Sonatas." *Music & Letters* 51 (1970), p. 51.

HORSLEY, IMOGENE. "Improvised Embellishment in the Performance of Renaissance Polyphonic Music." *JAMS* 4 (1951), p. 3.

HOWELL, ALMONTE. "Cabezón: An Essay in Structural Analysis." *MQ* 50 (1964), p. 18.
　　 "French Baroque Music and the Eight Church Tones." *JAMS* 11 (1959), p. 106.
　　 "Paired Imitation in the 16th-Century Spanish Keyboard Music." *MQ* 53 (1967), p. 377.

HUTCHINGS, ARTHUR. "The English Concerto with or for Organ." *MQ* 47 (1961): p. 195.

JACKSON, ROLAND. "On Frescobaldi's Chromaticism and Its Background." *MQ* 57 (1971), p. 255.

JEANS, SUSI. "The Pedal Clavichord and Other Practice Instruments of Organists." *PRMA* 77 (1950–1951), p. 1.

JONES, ESTHER. "Memoirs of Louis Vierne: His Life and Contacts with Famous Men," a translation. *The Diapason* (Sept. through Dec. 1938); (Jan. through July and later, 1939).

KASLING, KIM. "Some Editorial, Formal and Symbolic Aspects of J. S. Bach's Canonic Variations on 'Vom Himmel hoch da komm' ich her'." *The Diapason* (June 1971), p. 16; (Aug. 1971), p. 20.

KIRKPATRICK, RALPH. "Eighteenth Century Metronomic Indications." *Proceedings of the American Musicological Society* (1938), p. 30.

KLOPPERS, JACOBUS. "A Criterion for Manual Changes in the Organ Works of Bach," *The Organ Yearbook* (1976), p. 59.

KLOTZ, HANS. "The Organ Works of Max Reger: An Interpretation," *The Organ Yearbook* (1974), p. 66.

LEAVER, ROBIN. "Bach's *Clavierübung* III; Some Historical and Theological Considerations." *The Organ Yearbook* (1975), p. 17.

LESPINARD, BERNADETTE. *"L'Orgue Mystique* de Charles Tournemire." *L'Orgue* (Special Issue, II, 1971).

LONG, PAGE. "Vierne & His Six Organ Symphonies." *The Diapason* (June 1970), p. 23; (July 1970), p. 7; (Aug. 1970), p. 8.

MABRAY, RAYMOND. Arnolt Schlick and Tomás de Sancta Maria. Translation of the Prefaces by Kastner to editions of works by Schlick and Sancta Maria. *The Diapason* (Oct. 1972), p. 4.
　　 Translation of the Preface by Gesa Wolgast to the complete keyboard works of Georg Böhm, Vol. I. *The Diapason* (June 1972), p. 4.

MARCASE, DONALD. "Adriano Banchieri's L'Organo Suonarino." *The Diapason* (July 1973), p. 6; (Aug. 1973), p. 4; (Oct. 1973), p. 6.

MARCUSE, SIBYL. "Transposing Keyboards on Extant Flemish Harpsichords." *MQ* 38 (1952). p. 414.

MEEÙS, NICOLAS. "Some Hypotheses on the History of Organpitch before Schlick." *The Organ Yearbook* (1975), p. 42.

MILLER, HUGH W. "John Bull's Organ Works." *ML* 28 (1947), p. 25.
　　 "Sixteenth Century English Faburden Compositions for Keyboard." *MQ* 26 (1940), p. 50.

MULBURY, DAVID. "Bach's Passacaglia in C minor." *BACH*, (April 1972), p. 14; (Oct. 1972), p. 17.

NEUMANN, FREDERICK. "External Evidence and Uneven Notes." *MQ* 52 (1962), p. 448.

"The French Inégales, Quantz and Bach."
*JAMS* 18 (1965), p. 1. See also *JAMS* 20
(1967), p. 481.

NOLTE, EWALD. "The Magnificat Fugues of
Johann Pachelbel: Alternation or Intonation."
*JAMS* 9 (1956), p. 19.

PARKS, ANNE. "The Five Fantasies for Organ of
Ross Lee Finney." *The Diapason* (Dec. 1976),
p. 4.

PEETERS, F. "César Franck, Interpretation." *MUSIC
(A.G.O.)*, (Sept. 1971), p. 40.
        "The Organ Works of César Franck."
        *MUSIC (A.G.O.)*, (Aug. 1971), p. 22.

PETERSON, JOHN D. "Symbolism in J. S. Bach's
Prelude and Fugue in E-flat and its Effect on
Performance." *The Diapason*, (Feb. 1976),
p. 1.

PRINCE, PHILIP. "Reger and the Organ." *The
Diapason* (March 1973), p. 1.

PRUITT, WILLIAM. "Charles Tournemire & the Style
of Franck's Major Organ Works." *The Diapason* (Oct. 1970), p. 17.

SCHRADE, LEO. "The Organ in the Mass of the 15th
Century." *MQ* 28 (1942), p. 329.

SCHULZE, HANS-JOACHIM. "J. S. Bach's Concerto-
Arrangements for Organ—Studies or Commis-
sioned Works?" *The Organ Yearbook* (1972),
p. 4.

SCHUNEMAN, ROBERT. "Brahms and the Organ."
*MUSIC (A.G.O.)*, (Sept. 1972), p. 30.
        "The Organ Chorales of Georg Böhm." *The
        Diapason* (March 1970), p. 12.

SCHWEIGER, HERTHA. "Abt Vogler." *MQ* (1939).
p. 156.

SHACKELFORD, RUDY. "Analyses of Vincent Persichetti's Organ Works. *The Diapason* (beginning Sept., 1973 and continuing).

SHAY, EDMUND. "Eighteenth-Century Articulation:
A Guide." *MUSIC (A.G.O.)*, (March 1973),
p. 19.
        "The Expressive Use of Manual Changes in
        Bach's Six Great Preludes and Fugues."
        *The Diapason* (March 1968), p. 26;
        (May 1968), p. 24.

SIEBERT, F. MARK. "Mass Sections in the Buxheim
Organ Book." *MQ* 50 (1964), p. 353.

SPEER, KLAUS. "The Organ Verso in Iberian Music
up to 1700." *JAMS* 11 (1958), p. 189.

TAGLIAVINI, LUIGI. "The Old Italian Organ and Its
Music." *The Diapason* (Feb. 1966), p. 14.

THOMAS, W. R., and J. J. K. RHODES. "Schlick,
Praetorius and the History of Organ-Pitch."
*The Organ Yearbook* (1971), p. 58.

VANWYE, BENJAMIN. "Gregorian Influences in
French Organ Music before the *Motu Proprio*."
*JAMS* 27 (1974), p. 1.

WALTER, RUDOLF. "A Spanish Registration List of
c. 1770." *The Organ Yearbook* (1973), p. 40.

WILLIAMS, PETER. "J. S. Bach and English Organ
Music." *ML* 44 (1963), p. 140.
        "The Registration of Schitger's Organs." *The
        Organ* 47 (1968), p. 156.

WYLY, JAMES. "Registration of the Organ Works
of Francisco Correa de Arauxo." *Art of the
Organ* (Dec. 1971), p. 9.

YOUNG, CLYDE W. "Keyboard Music to 1600." *MD*
16 (1962), p. 115; 17 (1963), p. 163.

# Appendix E

## List of Illustrations

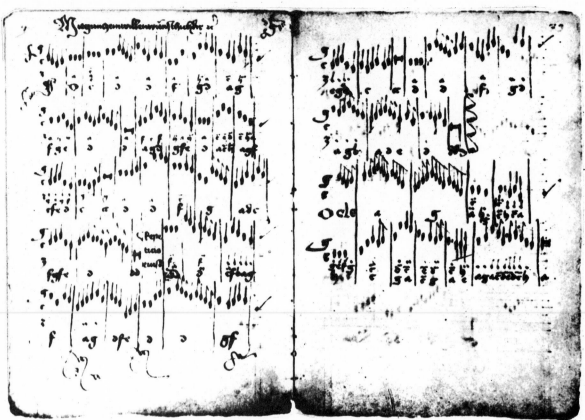

*Mit ganczen Willen* and *O cle* [mens] from Paumann's *Fundamentum organisandi* (1452).

Title page from Arnold Schlick's *Spiegel der Orgelmacher* (1511).

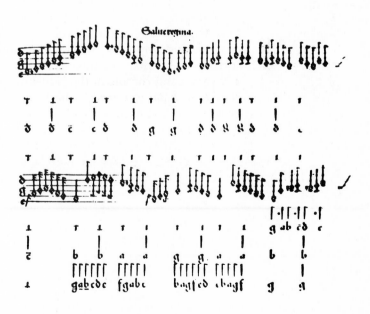

German organ tablature from Arnold Schlick's *Tablaturen etlicher lobegesang* (1512).

Woodcuts from Sebastian Virdung's *Musica getutscht* (1511), the first printed book on instruments in the German language.

Positiv and Regal. From Michael Praetorius' *Organographia* (1619).

Organ and console from Michael Praetorius' *Organographia* (1619).

The first *Toccata* from Girolamo Frescobaldi's *Toccate d' Intavolatura* (1637).

*Toccata XI* from Georg Muffat's *Apparatus musico-organisticus* (1690).

Organ built for the Dauphin, the father of Louis XVI, about 1748. It belonged at one time to Marie Antoinette and was played by Mozart at the Trianon.

The Totentanz Organ in the Marienkirche, Lübeck.

César Franck at the organ in Sainte-Clotilde.

The "Imperial Organ" (1549) in the Cathedral of Toledo, Spain.

The console of the organ in St. Bavo Kerk (1738), Haarlem, Holland.

302

SAINT-GERVAIS

The case and console of the organ in Saint-Gervais.

1723

1746

Portraits of J. S. Bach painted by Elias Gottlieb Haussman.

The organ and console in the Neuekirche, Arnstadt. J. S. Bach was the organist from 1703-1707.

*Prelude in E-flat* engraved by Bach. From the *Clavier-Übung*, III (1739).

*Praeambulum* from J. S. Bach's *Clavier-Büchlein vor W. F. Bach* (1720). The fingering is by J. S. Bach.

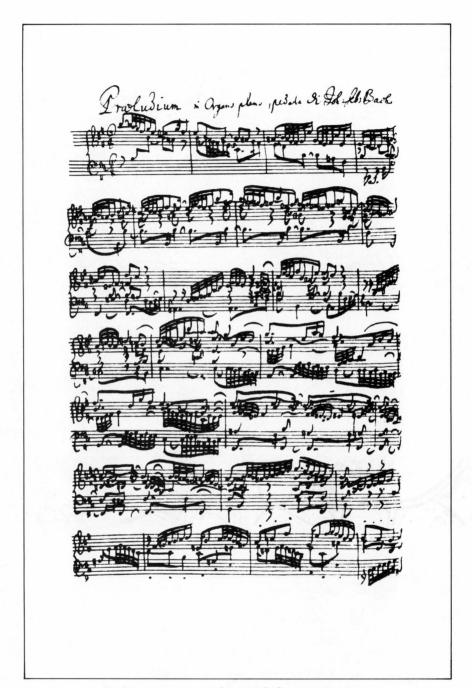

Bach's manuscript of his *Praeludium in B minor*.

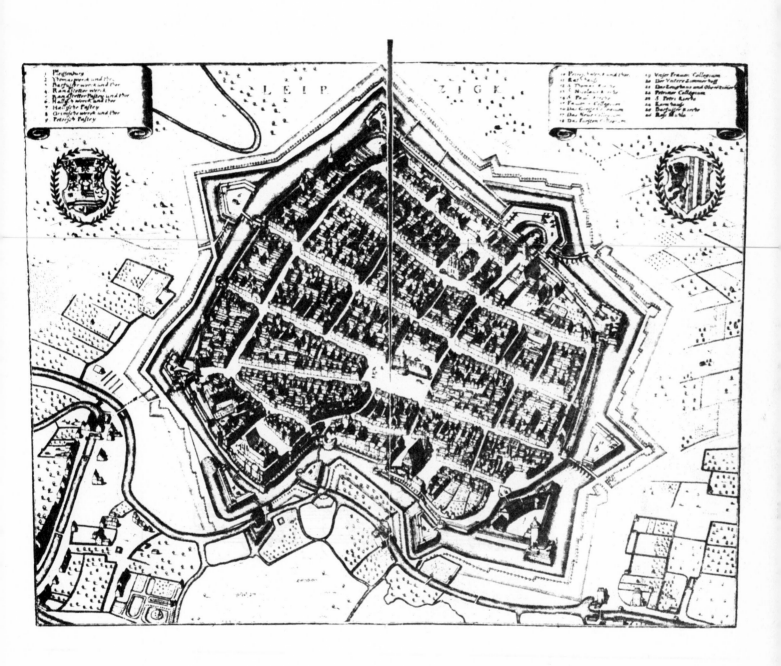

Leipzig, engraved by Matthaeus Merian (1652).

St. Thomaskirke is in the lower center near the river Pleisse.

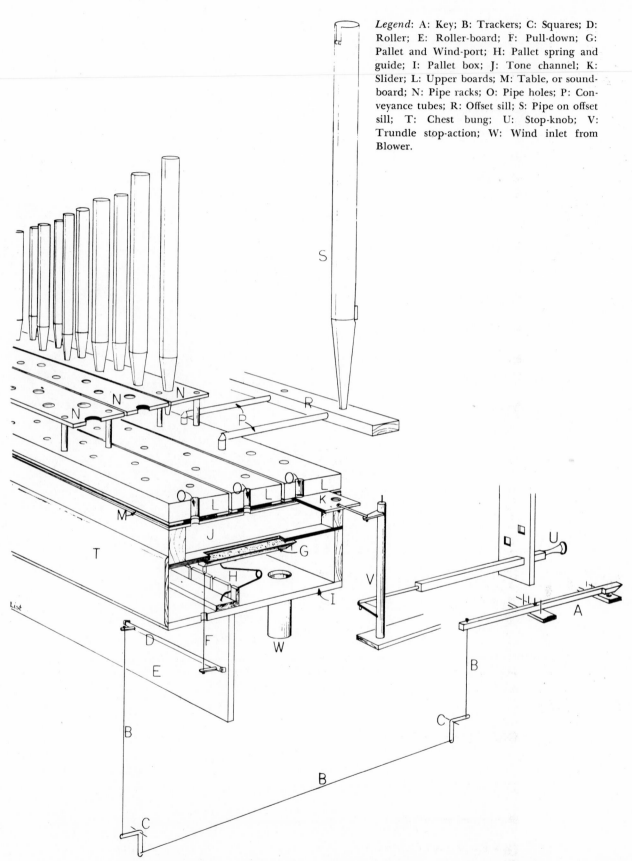

Diagram of mechanical organ key- and stop-action. (Lawrence Phelps and Associates, Erie, Pennsylvania)